Good Housekeeping
Consumer Guide

Your Family & the Law

Also available in the
CONSUMER GUIDE series

Home Security & Safety

Your Home & the Law

Buying & Selling Your Home

You & Your Rights

Your Family & Money

Good Housekeeping Consumer Guide

Your Family & the Law

Stephen Wildblood

EBURY PRESS · LONDON

The information in this book is believed to be correct at the time of going to press. Neither the author nor the publishers can accept any legal responsibility for any error or omission. If in doubt, always seek professional advice.

First published in 1996

1 3 5 7 9 10 8 6 4 2

Text copyright © Random House UK Ltd 1996

Stephen Wildblood has asserted his right to be identified as the author of this work.

All rights reserved. No part of this publication may be reproduced, stored in a retrieval system, or transmitted in any form or by any means, electronic, mechanical, photocopying, recording or otherwise, without the prior permission of the copyright owner.

The expression GOOD HOUSEKEEPING as used in the title of this book is the trade mark of the National Magazine Company Limited and the Hearst Corporation, registered in the United Kingdom and USA, and other principal countries of the world, and is the absolute property of the National Magazine Company Limited and the Hearst Corporation. The use of this trade mark other than with the express permission of the National Magazine Company Limited or the Hearst Corporation is strictly prohibited.

First published in the United Kingdom in 1996 by
Ebury Press · Random House · 20 Vauxhall Bridge Road · London SW1V 2SA

Random House Australia (Pty) Limited
20 Alfred Street · Milsons Point · Sydney · New South Wales 2061 · Australia

Random House New Zealand Limited
18 Poland Road · Glenfield
Auckland 10 · New Zealand

Random House South Africa (Pty) Limited
PO Box 337 · Bergvlei · South Africa

Random House UK Limited Reg. No. 954009

A CIP catalogue record for this book is available from the British Library.

Editor: Melanie Sensicle
Design: Martin Lovelock

ISBN: 0 09 181304 2

Printed and bound in Great Britain by Mackays of Chatham plc. Kent

Contents

Introduction	7
1. Marriage and Cohabitation	9
2. Violence, Injunctions and the Home	21
3. Divorce, Separation and Nullity	31
4. Finances	45
5. Property Issues between Cohabitees	67
6. Financial Arrangements for Children	73
7. The Children Act – 'Private Law'	83
8. The Children Act – 'Public Law'	95
9. Adoption and Fostering	103
10. What Happens on Death?	111
11. Legal Costs	117
Glossary	123
Useful Addresses	132
Index	137

Introduction

Most people regard their immediate and extended family as central to their happiness. However, as expectations and the speed of life increase, so the family has come under increased pressure.

The consequence, in this country, has been that we now have one of the highest divorce rates in western society and it is still growing. Although more people are now choosing not to marry, living together can carry with it at least as many complications as marriage.

In an ideal world families would provide the security to permit happiness and development for its individual members. When families break down there is inevitable sadness and insecurity. Some of that sadness and insecurity is caused by uncertainty about the consequences of such a breakdown: what happens to the children; what happens to the home and any available finance?

Although the family is often thought of as a simple domestic arrangement, some of the most demanding problems arise out of it. Finances are often limited and may be tied up in the home or a business; new partners may become involved; a web of problems may arise over children.

No book, even a legal textbook – which this is not – can provide a simple answer to family problems. The purpose of this book is to give a straightforward account of some of the main legal aspects of family life and breakdown.

The best preliminary advice, whether on legal or emotional issues, must be to seek advice before things get too entangled. Although the courts are generally available to resolve any disagreements, going to court is expensive and can prove demeaning. The emphasis now is on encouraging people to resolve their own difficulties, with the aid, if necessary, of appropriate advice.

CHAPTER 1
Marriage and Cohabitation

Your rights within a relationship

WHAT IS A MARRIAGE?

Although people often speak about a 'common law husband/wife', the law of England and Wales does not recognise that there is such a thing as a 'common law marriage'. People are either married or they are not as far as the law is concerned.

Although the marriage ceremony has to follow legal requirements, the definition of a marriage most frequently used since 1866 is 'a voluntary union for life of one man and one woman to the exclusion of all others'. Bigamy still remains a serious offence and may have serious financial consequences when the marriage is either ended or declared a nullity. With the advent of today's multi-cultural society, some recognition has been given to polygamous marriages but such recognition is limited.

This chapter looks at the rights and responsibilities that arise when people live together as man and wife, married or not. In particular it considers:
- the position concerning children whilst the family remains intact
- the position concerning the home
- the particular rights of married people.

MARRIED PEOPLES' RIGHTS

For very many years the law has given rights to married people some of which are exclusive to them.

Those rights include :
- the right to be properly maintained within the ambit of the available resources
- the right not to be excluded from the family home, unless this is ordered by a court
- shared parental responsibility for children irrespective of the conflicting wishes of the spouses.

MAINTENANCE

It is well recognised in law that spouses may be forced to maintain each other, a duty which extends to both husbands and wives. If a spouse fails to maintain the other, an application can be made to the court for maintenance or a lump sum (ie a capital sum).

When marriages get into difficulties it is very easy for the finances to get neglected. This may put a home at risk if, for instance, the mortgage is not being paid. It may be necessary to consider asking the court to make an order for maintenance or a lump sum to protect the family whilst the long-term future is being decided.

Financial orders while the marriage still legally exists are usually dealt with either in the county court or in the magistrates' court.

The magistrates' court and maintenance

In the magistrates' court the case is started by a written application to the court. When considering whether to make an order, and the amount to be ordered, the court has to take into account and makes its assessment according to the following criteria:
- the financial position of the parties
- their respective needs, obligations and responsibilities
- the standard of living of the family
- the age of the parties and the duration of the marriage
- any disabilities of either party
- the contributions of the parties to the marriage, including any contributions in looking after the family

- the conduct of the parties where the court thinks that it would be inequitable to disregard that conduct, (this is rare).

The magistrates court can only make limited orders for lump sums up to £1,000.

The county court and maintenance

In the county court the proceedings are started by an application. The parties file affidavits setting out their arguments and financial resources. The advantage of the county court procedure, as opposed to that of the magistrates' court, is that both parties can get more advance notice of the other's arguments before going to court because the court can order that documents be disclosed.

Usually the purpose of a maintenance or lump sum award will be to ensure that the family does not suffer unnecessarily during a period of difficulty.

RIGHTS OF OCCUPATION OF THE HOME

Before 1967 a person's right to occupy a house depended entirely on whose name the house was in and the other aspects of the general law relating to property. After 1967 an Act of Parliament gave both spouses the right to live in the home irrespective of whose name the house was in except where a court had ordered to the contrary. The law still provides these rights and will continue to do so if the proposed amendments to the law under The Family Law Bill are implemented (see Chapter 2)

Since 1976, in those cases where unmarried people have been 'living together as man and wife' they have been able to ask the court to make orders to bring about the following:
- to prevent a partner from being violent towards them or from pestering them
- to make a partner leave the home or a part of it
- to allow the applicant to occupy the home.

To an extent this is similar to the rights of married people. These rights are considered in more detail in the next chapter.

RESPONSIBILITY FOR CHILDREN

The many legal issues that can arise concerning children are considered in more depth in Chapters 7 and 8 which look specifically at The Children Act 1989 and how it affects private and public law. In this chapter, as a starting point, attention is given to the responsibility that parents have to their children whilst the family is intact.

When parents are married, they each have parental responsibility for the children of the marriage. If the marriage breaks down, they will both continue to retain that parental responsibility.

When parents are not married, the law states that only the mother has parental responsibility for the children. Although there is still an expectation that parents will discuss with each other matters relating to the children, the person with parental responsibility is recognised in legal terms, as having the greater responsibility for the child. This obviously leaves unmarried fathers at a potential disadvantage.

Where two parents have parental responsibility it means that the law recognises them as having an equal status and responsibility for the child concerned, unless their responsibilities are otherwise defined or limited by an order of the court. Parental responsibility may be of importance, for instance, when consent has to be given for medical treatment or where questions arise about schooling, religion, consent to marriage or, even, emigration.

It is expected that those parents with shared parental responsibility will discuss between themselves any issues that may arise in respect of their children, for neither of them has the legal right to dominate the wishes of the other.

Parental responsibility and unmarried fathers

The disadvantage that unmarried fathers have under the law can be redressed in two ways:
- by means of a parental responsibility agreement which is a written agreement (that has to be recorded in a prescribed way) between the parents giving the father parental responsibility
- by a court ordering that the father is to have parental responsibility.

Parental responsibility agreement This has to be in the shape of a prescribed form which can be obtained from most law centres, courts or solicitors. The contents of the form are laid down by regulations. If you need a form, try ringing your local magistrates court – new forms were introduced in January 1995 so make sure that you get the right one. On the forms it is necessary to:
- set out the name of the child or children
- set out the names and addresses of the parents
- ensure the agreement is signed by the parents and by official witnesses (eg a justice of the peace, a justices clerk, or an officer of the county court or high court who is authorised to administer oaths). In order for someone to witness the agreement you will need to contact your local court and make arrangements for this to be done.

Court orders for parental responsibility These are considered in more detail in Chapter 7. However, it is worth mentioning here that it is rare for a court to refuse to make a parental responsibility order where a father applies for it. In deciding whether to make such an order, the court will take into account :
- the father's attachment to the child
- the father's commitment to the child
- the reasons for the father's application, ie whether it is out of attachment and commitment to the child, or, for instance, is part of a campaign against the mother.

Generally a court will regard it as in the interests of a child that both of the child's parents are fully recognised as parents.

Step-parents and parental responsibility
Step-parents do not have parental responsibility for step-children nor can they acquire it by agreement or by seeking a parental responsibility order from the court. They will acquire parental responsibility if a residence order in respect of the child is made in their favour or if they adopt the child. Step-parents have greater rights to in seeking orders from the court

in respect of step-children than members of the more extended family such as aunts, uncles or grandparents (see Chapter 9).

Parents liability for the actions of children

There is no absolute rule that parents are liable for any 'tort' or civil wrong committed by their child that causes damage to others. However a parent may be liable for the wrongs of a child where:
- the parent fails to exercise proper supervision of a child, for example an unruly child running out into the road and causing a collision
- The parent allows the child charge of a dangerous object when harm to others is reasonably foreseeable, for example a loaded gun.

Committing a tort will usually lead to damages and/or the granting of an injunction. An example of such a tort is the tort of negligence (eg the first of the above examples).

Where a child is convicted or found guilty of a criminal act and the punishment for the offence is a fine, costs or compensation, a court can order that the fine, costs or compensation are paid by a parent.

THE HOME

When the question of ownership of the home is raised between married people where the marriage remains intact, the legal position is determined by the same general law that applies to any other two people who live together. There are some small differences for married people; they go through slightly different legal procedures and married people may find it easier to claim a legal share in a house owned in the name of the other spouse where they have made substantial contributions to the improvement of the property.

Generally, though, married peoples' rights of ownership of the home are governed by the law relating to property while the marriage survives and while there are no applications to the court for financial provision in respect of children.

A court may alter existing property rights under the following circumstances:

- after a divorce, judicial separation or decree of nullity of marriage
- in proceedings where financial provision is sought for the benefit of a child under Schedule One of the Children Act 1989 (see Chapter 6).

Property owned by more than one person

When people live together they will often chose to own the home jointly. By law this means that the home is held by them as trustees of a trust affecting the home. Technically the trust is described as a trust for sale which means that, in most circumstances, if the joint owners cannot agree whether the property is to be kept or sold, a sale will take place unless the court orders otherwise. Obviously there are many circumstances where the court will say that the home shouldn't be sold, particularly in divorce proceedings or where there are children living in the home.

Under a trust a person's shares in the property are called the ' beneficial interests'.

There are two legal bases upon which the beneficial interests in a property may be held by more than one person:

1 Beneficial joint tenants This means that the owners are each regarded as owning the whole of the property and, on death, the share of the dead owner passes automatically to the surviving owner by operation of law. In legal terms this is called the 'right of survivorship'.

Where property is held by beneficial joint tenants, it is possible for them to 'sever' the joint tenancy by a 'notice of severance' which is sent by one owner to the other owner(s) and expresses the wish to sever the joint tenancy. The effect of this is that, unless otherwise agreed between the owners, they become '**tenants in common**' with equal shares in the property. When they die their shares will pass under their wills or the law of intestacy.

2 Beneficial tenants in common This means that the owners each have a specific share in the property, eg a half, a third, a quarter. On the death of one owner the survivor does not automatically get the other share; it passes to whoever is the beneficiary under the terms of the dead person's will or by the law of intestacy. The size of a tenant in common's share will be determined by the title deeds to the property or other provisions of the general law relating to property and trusts.

If the property is held in the sole name of one person and there is no formal document declaring that someone else has a share in it, the property will obviously belong to the person in whose name it was originally bought unless someone else can claim a share in it under the general law relating to property.

GENERAL LAW RELATING TO PROPERTY

Where two or more people claim to own property, it is usually necessary to apply the general law relating to property in order to decide what the owners' property rights are.

If the proportion of the property owned by each person is laid down in the title deeds of the property, those documents are likely to be treated as definitive.

If the deeds are silent about who owns what – or if the property was bought in the sole name of one person and someone else wants to claim a share or 'beneficial interest' in it, it will be necessary to discover the following:

- What the parties expressly agreed, arranged or understood between themselves about the ownership of the property at the time of purchase. If there was a specific, expressed (ie communicated) agreement, arrangement or understanding between the parties and the person claiming an interest acted upon it (for example spent money on the property) the property is likely to be considered as owned in the agreed shares.
- Who paid what towards the purchase of the property? Who paid the initial deposit on the property or the mortgage? If both parties paid towards the property their shares in the property will usually be decided according to the percentage of the purchase price that they paid, subject to any contrary agreement.

Similar rules apply to 'personal property', a legal term meaning property that is not land or buildings – such as furniture, a car, or even the pets. There are special rules relating to wedding gifts and engagement rings.

Sale of a property
Once the legal position on ownership is established, and if the result is that two people have a share in a property, the question often arises whether the home should be sold. The general rule is that where one owner objects to the sale of the home, a court will not order a sale if to do so would be contrary to the original purpose for which the property was bought, for example as a home for the family, including the children. If the home is only used by two adult cohabitees, a court will usually order a sale. Different rules apply in divorce cases and in cases where financial provision is sought for a child.

Sorting it out at the start
Joint owners need to decide how they wish to own, or 'hold', a property when it is purchased. The options should be discussed with care with any solicitor who is acting for you on the purchase. If you don't have a solicitor you need to decide for yourselves. Bear in mind the following:
- On separation, the rights of unmarried people will usually be decided by the title deeds to the property. These documents are important.
- Married people and, to a lesser extent, people with children who make applications for financial provision for the benefit of the children have the right to ask the court to vary the strict legal ownership of the home by making a property adjustment order.
- If you are joint tenants and one of you dies the other will automatically get the dead person's share, unless the joint tenancy is severed.
- If you split up and sever the joint tenancy, you and your partner will probably hold the property in equal shares.
- If you agree that you should be tenants in common with specified shares in the property, this may leave one of you vulnerable on the death of the other or after the relationship has gone on for a long time.

THE FAMILY HOME

Mortgages and charges

The family home is often the main capital asset that a couple will own. As such it is often suggested that the home should be used as security for raising money. Although this may seem like an attractive proposition it can lead to disaster. Sometimes the home is taken by a bank as security for all indebtedness that the couple have to that bank without any limitation (for example where a bank is lending money to support a business). Anyone signing such an agreement, or 'charge', needs to think very carefully indeed about what they are doing and should bear in mind the following:

- Don't rush into signing it.
- Take professional advice from a solicitor. Make sure that you know what you are signing.
- Consider agreeing a limit, or ceiling, to the amount that can be secured against the home. For example, only borrow the actual amount needed to set up a business – if it proves necessary to borrow more at alater date you may be able to renegotiate the limit with the lender.
- Remember that if the relationship between you and your partner should break down it will probably not be possible to get the charge removed from the home, even by a court order.
- Remember that the bank could force the sale of the home if the debt repayments are not made.

If the home is in your partner's sole name and you suspect that your partner is trying to sell or get a charge put on the home against your wishes, you need to take steps quickly to stop the sale or charge. Go immediately to a solicitor and take his or her advice. If you are married it may well be that you are able to register your rights with the land registry (which is there to notify prospective buyers and mortgagees, eg a building society, of the rights of others in the property). Otherwise you may need to go to court to ask for an injunction in order to prevent your partner from taking those steps.

Bankruptcy

If your partner goes bankrupt all his or her assets will 'vest' in the 'official receiver' or the 'trustee in bankruptcy'. This means that an official takes over your partner's affairs and such a duty can extend to belongings (with certain exceptions) in order to pay off the creditors. If this happens it is again important to establish quickly what is yours and what is your partner's. The general law will be applied to determine who owns what, whether you are married or unmarried (with only limited exceptions). Although a court can help in deciding who owns what, it cannot take away from the official receiver or trustee things that belong to your partner.

If your partner goes bankrupt any beneficial joint tenancy is automatically severed, so that the official receiver or trustee takes an equal share in the property with the other owners.

PRE-MARRIAGE AND PRE-COHABITATION AGREEMENTS

There is a growing trend for people to try to make agreements that will avoid disputes or limit the scope for argument if the relationship breaks down. Agreements are often made on financial matters, to decide who gets what. They can relate to the home or other buildings or land.

Agreements between married people

In the case of married and divorced people it is well established in law that the court's jurisdiction to decide financial issues in cases of divorce, judicial separation or nullity cannot be ousted by an agreement. The court still decides who gets what, although it may attach considerable importance to an agreement between a married couple when making a decision, depending on the circumstances in which it was made. For instance, if a wife agreed before her marriage that all the capital belonged to her future husband, a court might ignore the agreement if, by the time the matter came to court, there were four children to be considered or the couple had been married for some time and the wife had invested all her money into the home.

Agreements between unmarried couples

The position is more complicated. When unmarried people separate, the court does not have the same powers as it does for married couples, and agreements, therefore, may have much more influence on deciding who owns what. If unmarried partners are considering making a formal agreement between themselves about the ownership of their property or possessions, it is important that they take legal advice before making the agreement. This is particularly relevant when considering the family home.

If an agreement is made, it might be regarded as unenforceable (in the same way that any contract may be rendered unenforceable) on the basis of:
- Fraud (ie deceit)
- Duress
- Undue influence
- Misrepresentation.

CHAPTER 2

Violence, Injunctions and the Home

The home is the setting for more violence than any other environment. As society has become more prepared to recognise the extent of the problem that domestic violence represents, so the methods for preventing it have increased. This chapter examines various ways in which the law seeks to curb domestic violence. It also examines how the occupation of the family home may be regulated by the court.

VIOLENCE AS A CRIME

Violence in the home is as much a crime as violence elsewhere. Perpetrators of domestic violence are prosecuted under the same criminal law as perpetrators of violence in other any other circumstances. A range of offences is available as a framework for the prosecution of violent offenders. The specific offence with which someone may be charged depends on the seriousness of the injury inflicted. The range includes:

- **Common assault** – an assault is any act by which a person intentionally or recklessly causes another person to suffer or apprehend immediate and unlawful violence. The act has to be accompanied by a hostile intent but does not have to cause bodily harm. The maximum prison sentence is six months.

- **Assault occasioning actual bodily harm** – this is any assault that results in bodily harm to the victim. Bodily harm includes any hurt or injury which interferes with the health or comfort of the victim. The maximum prison sentence is five years.

- **Unlawfully and maliciously wounding or inflicting grievous bodily harm (with or without a weapon)** – the maximum prison sentence is five years.

- **Unlawfully and maliciously wounding or causing grievous bodily harm with intent to do some grievous bodily harm (GBH with intent)** – the maximum prison sentence is life imprisonment.

In addition there are specific recognised offences in those cases when violence is perpetrated against a child, such as cruelty to a child.

Rape

Until 1991 it was assumed that a husband could not be accused of raping his wife. However in a landmark judgement in 1992 the House of Lords ruled that a husband could commit this offence against a wife. Since then a number of husbands have been sentenced to prison for rape. The length of sentence obviously depends on the facts of the case; prison sentences in 1992 included one of 6 years and one of 5 years.

This ruling applies equally to cohabitees: rape or assault against a cohabitee is a criminal offence.

Since 1986 the police have been able to compel a wife to give evidence against her husband where the husband is suspected of domestic violence. However, where a spouse is forced against his or her wishes, to give evidence against the other spouse, prosecutions may prove difficult to justify or sustain.

Women may not want to give evidence for reasons such as: not wanting to precipitate a divorce or family breakdown; fear of reprisals; or a false feeling that they are partly responsible for the violence.

If violence goes unchecked it can all too easily escalate and become accepted as normal within a relationship, which in turn can lead to someone being badly hurt. It does little to deter domestic violence if the perpetrator is taken to court but escapes prosecution because the main witness, the perpetrator's cohabitee or spouse, refuses to give evidence at the hearing.

VIOLENCE AS A CIVIL WRONG

The legal word used to describe civil wrongs is 'tort'. It comes from the French word meaning 'wrong'. Violence is referred to as the tort of 'assault and battery'. Other torts are negligence (eg being at fault in a crash), nuisance (eg keeping your neighbours awake by having wild parties every night) and trespass.

The civil courts control torts by awarding damages and/or making injunctions.

Damages

The word 'damages' is the legal term for monetary compensation. The more serious the harm, the larger the award of damages will be. However, most people suffering violence from a family member are not particularly interested in being awarded damages, because damages simply make things financially worse for the rest of the family. The main reason for taking legal action is to stop the violence.

Injunctions and undertakings

Injunctions (see Glossary on page 124 for a full definition) are granted by a court where violence has taken place between parties and are frequently used to regulate the occupation of the family home when a relationship is breaking down.

The person applying for the injunction is called the **applicant**; the person on whom it is served, who has to respond to the injunction, is called the **respondent**.

People often fear going to court. When a relationship breaks down most people do not want the added pressure of court proceedings. However, the reality is that in most cases where injunctions are sought proceedings get no further than a preliminary court hearing because the people involved are able to agree on how to proceed, ie the violent person promises to stop behaving in the way that has prompted the complaint. Promises of this type are called 'undertakings'. They are formal promises to the court, not simply promises to the other party.

Injunctions and undertakings are enforced in exactly the same way; both contain a penal notice (see Glossary on page 124 for exact wording) warning the person at fault that if they break an injunction or undertaking they may be sent to prison.

Because there are many specific remedies under Acts of Parliament concerning violence between spouses, former spouses, cohabitees and former cohabitees, that allow injunctions to be made without having to rely on the general civil law, people rarely apply for damages and injunctions under the civil law of tort in order to prevent violence.

Circumstances where a civil action based on tort is the only way of getting an injunction are:
- where an unmarried couple have been living apart for some time before the violence by one of them occurred
- where violence occurs between a homosexual couple
- where a member of the extended family is being subjected to violence. For example, where a person is being assaulted by an adult child, or where an adult enters his parents' house against their wishes (which is trespass).

Interim or interlocutory injunctions The advantage of civil actions is that it is possible to get the matter before the court quickly and prevent wrongs continuing at an earlier stage of legal proceedings when the main court hearing will not occur for sometime. These are known as interim or interlocutory injunctions.

'Ex parte' injunctions In cases of emergency, the court may grant 'ex parte' injunctions which are granted without the other party being present or being given notice of the hearing.

VIOLENCE BETWEEN COHABITEES AND MARRIED PEOPLE

Under the existing law a married person or a person who is living with a partner of the opposite sex 'as husband and wife' may seek an injunction under an Act of Parliament specifically designed to deter domestic violence. Married people can apply to the magistrates' court, the county court or the high court (cohabitees can apply to the county court or high court). Each form of injunction is examined in more detail below. However, it must be remembered that these provisions may be amended by new legislation in the future. For example if the Family Law Bill is passed (see page 27 for a summary of the suggested amendments).

Injunctions ordered by county or high court

Only in very rare cases will injunctions be used to settle long-term arrangements following separation. Married people or people who are living together as husband and wife can apply to the county court or high court for:

- Injunctions preventing the other person from 'molesting' the applicant or a child living with the applicant. The use of the word 'molest' is unfortunate because of its sexual connotations. In the context of domestic injunctions it means 'pester' and does not bear any sexual overtones. Examples of 'molestation' would be following someone down the street in a threatening way, making nuisance telephone calls or throwing stones at the windows. Having said that, molestation also includes physical and sexual assault and harassment.
- Injunctions excluding the other person from the home (ouster injunctions) or a specified area in which the home is situated.
- Injunctions requiring the other person to permit the applicant to enter and remain in the home (or a part of the home).

Ouster injunctions An order requiring a spouse or former cohabitee to leave the home is regarded as draconian and should only be made if no lesser measure would adequately protect the applicant or the children. This is because it is thought to be wrong to remove someone from his or her home, unless there are strong reasons to do so, until the court is in a position to decide the full financial issues between the parties.

In deciding whether to order a person out of the home, the court will look at all the circumstances of the case and, in particular, the conduct of the people involved, their needs and financial resources and the needs of any children. However, the welfare of children is **not** the paramount consideration when a court is asked to order an ouster injunction. Very often the focus is on the conduct of the partners involved and their housing needs.

Attaching powers of arrest to an injunction Where the court is satisfied that one party has caused 'actual bodily harm' to the applicant or a child living with the applicant and is likely to do so again, the court may attach a power of arrest to an injunction between spouses or cohabitees if the injunction is an 'ouster' injunction or if it orders the violent party not to use violence against the applicant or a child.

The effect of a power of arrest is that a person who is suspected of being in breach of an injunction can be arrested without a warrant. The arrested person has to be brought before a judge within 24 hours of the arrest.

Injunctions ordered by a magistrates' court
Only married people are entitled to apply to the magistrates' court for injunctions. Magistrates' courts have more limited powers than those possessed by the county and high courts. They can make the following orders for married people:

Personal protection orders These say that the respondent shall not use or threaten violence against the applicant or a child of the family. Personal protection orders will only be made in cases where it is proved that there have been acts or threats of violence against the applicant or a child of the family.

Exclusion orders These require the respondent to leave the matrimonial home; they may also prohibit the respondent from entering that home. An exclusion order may be granted if the magistrates' court is satisfied on one

of the following grounds:
- the respondent has used violence against the applicant or a child of the family
- the respondent has threatened violence against the applicant or a child of the family in breach of a personal protection order
- the respondent has threatened violence and used it against someone else and, in any event, that the applicant or child of the family is in danger of being physically injured by the respondent or would be in danger if the applicant or child were to enter the home.

Punishment

A person who breaches an injunction or undertaking is guilty of a contempt of court and as a result may be fined or sent to prison. Where a breach of an injunction or undertaking is alleged, the person alleging the breach brings 'committal' proceedings. These are formal proceedings which require that the breach be formally proved to the criminal standard of proof, which means a judge must be satisfied beyond reasonable doubt that the alleged breaches have occurred. Serious breaches will result in heavy penalties in addition to any criminal prosecutions that may be brought as a result. Minor breaches may be punished with suspended prison sentences or fines, the exact punishsment depending on the facts of the individual case.

Alterations in the law: the Family Law Bill

The law relating to injunctions may alter under the Family Law Bill. This now incorporates provisions that were originally in the Family Homes and Domestic Violence Bill, which was widely expected to be passed by Parliament at the end of 1995 and implemented quickly. The Bill was intended to simplify the law and extend the range of individuals who would be entitled to seek injunctions to include relatives and former cohabitants. However, Parliament decided not to pass the bill as it then stood, although some of the proposals have reappeared in the proposed amendments to the divorce law (see Chapter 3, pages 42-3). Therefore the present legal provisions remain in force.

HOW TO GET TO COURT

Most people will want to be legally represented at injunction hearings. If you chose to represent yourself it is worth ensuring that:
- You know where the court is located – telephone the court on the day before
- You know the time of the hearing and arrive in good time
- Any witnesses attend on time.

In order to prepare your case for court a solicitor will need to have as much background information as possible. An application for an injunction is made in writing. The written document sets out the orders that are being sought. Usually injunctions have to be heard 'on notice', which means that the responding party has advance notice of the hearing date and the right to attend the hearing and give evidence.

In the county court, the applicant and any witnesses file affidavits giving evidence of what has been happening. The respondent may file a cross application and affidavits. In magistrates' courts the hearing is largely on oral evidence.

Your solicitor will have to know why it is necessary to seek the injunction and whether it is necessary to make an emergency application for an ex parte injunction (see below). If you can it is worth going to the solicitor with something in writing setting out the brief facts of what has been happening.

In court you will have to substantiate what you have said on paper, in any affidavit or application. It is therefore very important that you give an accurate written account.

Where it is necessary to obtain an order as an emergency, an **ex parte injunction** may be sought (ie an order obtained in the absence of the other person).

WHAT HAPPENS WHEN YOU GET THERE

The hearing of the application may be before the magistrates or before a judge. Magistrates and district judges are addressed as 'sir' or 'madam'.

Circuit judges are addressed as 'your honour'. To find out who you are appearing in front of it is worth checking with your solicitor or the court usher.

The procedure in court, if a case remains contested, is as follows:
1 The case begins with the applicant or the applicant's representative giving an 'opening', a brief summary of the case.
2 The applicant's evidence is 'called' which involves the applicant going into the witness box. The applicant first gives 'evidence in chief' which means a response to questions from his or her own representative. An applicant representing himself is asked to give his version of events. Evidence in chief is followed by cross examination, which involves the applicant answering questions put by the respondent or the respondent's representative.
3 Next comes re-examination, which involves the applicant (or the applicant's representative) asking questions on matters that arose during cross examination.
4 The applicant or his representative calls witnesses to give evidence. Those witnesses are then cross-examined and re-examined.
5 The same procedure, steps 1-4, is adopted for the respondent.
6 The respondent has the opportunity to make a speech to the judge.
7 The applicant makes a speech.
8 The judge or magistrate gives a judgement, explaining what they are going to order and why the order is going to be made.

Giving evidence
The knack to giving evidence is:
- listen to the question that is asked
- answer the question as best you can
- speak clearly and briefly.

After injunction proceedings in cases where people are married, the next stage may well be divorce or some other formal proceedings to recognise the end of the marriage. This procedure is described in the next chapter.

CHAPTER 3
Divorce, Separation and Nullity

When a marriage breaks down there is an inevitable starting point to the process of formal separation and divorce and this point is often the most difficult for the people involved, including the children. The person who initiates the process of separation may feel very unsure whether it is the best thing to do. Both people are likely to feel hurt; the children are likely to feel unhappy and unsettled.

Therefore, if two people separate and/or divorce it is important that the process should be made as smooth as possible. This chapter examines the process by which divorce, judicial separation and nullity of marriage are effected.

WHEN IS A MARRIAGE LEGALLY ENDED?

When a marriage breaks down, there are two ways of getting legal recognition of the break down; these are judicial separation and divorce. In certain limited circumstances, it may be possible for a marriage to be declared a nullity, but this third possibility is a rare way for the marriage to be recognised as being at an end (see page 35).

The person initiating proceedings in all three of the above methods is called the **petitioner**; the person who receives the petition is called the **respondent**.

JUDICIAL SEPARATION

When married partners are judicially separated, they remain married. The purpose of judicial separation is to give formal recognition to a separation without ending the marriage. There are many reasons why someone may choose this method. For example:

- the petitioner may hope for a reconciliation, whilst at the same time wanting legal orders relating to finances and, possibly, the children
- it may be financially disadvantageous to get divorced, for example if an insurance policy or a pension exists under which the petitioner wants to be able to claim as a widow/widower or spouse rather than a 'former spouse' (both people remain spouses after a judicial separation)
- it can prevent a spouse from getting remarried while still taking action over the marriage. Judicial separation can be used in this way, although this may cause ill-feeling and usually only holds up a divorce which may be obtained later by the person who wants to remarry.

In order to get a decree of judicial separation, it is not necessary to prove or state that the marriage has broken down irretrievably. The grounds for judicial separation are, otherwise, the same as the grounds for divorce (ie adultery, behaviour, desertion, two years living apart and consent, or 5 years apart. See below).

DIVORCE

What is a divorce?

A divorce is a court order which brings a marriage to an end; the marriage is 'dissolved'. This process happens in two stages, first the court makes a preliminary order called a 'decree nisi' and then the marriage is formally ended by a 'decree absolute'.

There is still a degree of technicality about the basis for a divorce which has led to a thorough review of the divorce law. Proposals for reform have been made in a recent government 'White Paper': *Looking to the Future. Mediation and the ground for divorce* which was issued in April 1995. These proposals are now incorporated in the Family Law Bill. The proposals in the Bill are considered at the end of this chapter (see pages 42-3).

The grounds of divorce

The only legal basis for a divorce is that the marriage has broken down irretrievably. However the only legal grounds upon which it can be proved that a marriage has broken down irretrievably are one or more of the following:

- The respondent has committed adultery and the petitioner finds it intolerable to live with the respondent
- The respondent has behaved in such a way that the petitioner cannot reasonably be expected to live with the respondent
- The respondent has deserted the petitioner for a continuous period of at least two years immediately preceding the presentation of the petition
- The parties to the marriage have lived apart for a continuous period of at least two years immediately preceding the presentation of the petition and the respondent consents to a decree being granted
- The parties to the marriage have lived apart for a continuous period of at least five years immediately preceding the presentation of the petition.

Adultery and behaviour are the grounds most commonly used probably because the others can involve considerable delay.

Occasionally people decide to try to get a divorce on false grounds, for example by saying that they have lived apart for two years when this has not been the case. This is a serious mistake and inevitably leads to someone having to lie to the court. Such deception usually amounts to a criminal offence, because it involves lying in a sworn affidavit (see the Glossary on page 125 for a full definition). Not just the petitioner but also the respondent may be guilty of a criminal offence. A divorce obtained on false grounds could later be set aside by the court. The moral is, don't be tempted to do it.

Adultery

Adultery is voluntary sexual intercourse between a man and a woman who are not married to each other but one of whom is married to another person. Sexual activity other than sexual intercourse amount to adultery. There has to be some element of penetration by the man, although completed intercourse is not necessary. Other forms of sexual activity would, in most marriages, satisfy the requirement that 'the respondent's behaviour has been such that the petitioner cannot reasonably be expected to live with the respondent'.

If adultery is proved in an undefended case, it is presumed that the petitioner finds it intolerable to live with the respondent.

In some marriages adultery is tolerated, particularly where there is an 'open' marriage agreement. It would be somewhat bizarre if a marriage could be ended on the basis of an act of adultery years after that act which had been well known at the time. Therefore the law states that, if the married couple live together for more than six months after the adultery became known, that act cannot be relied upon as grounds for a divorce.

Behaviour

For a divorce to be made on the ground of what is often termed 'unreasonable behaviour', the following issues must be examined:
- how the respondent has behaved (what he/she has done)
- the effect of that behaviour on the petitioner
- would a right thinking person conclude that the behaviour of the respondent is such that this petitioner cannot reasonably be expected to live with this respondent?

Sometimes people refer to 'mental cruelty' as a ground for divorce; in fact, it is not a ground although it would, in most cases, amount to unreasonable behaviour.

What happens when two people continue to live under the same roof following an incident that forms the basis for divorce on the ground of behaviour because, for example, neither of them is able to make other arrangements for alternative accommodation? Should this be taken into consideration when deciding whether the person seeking the divorce can reasonably be expected to live with the other party? It depends on how long they have continued to live together after the incident. If it is under six months, their living together must be disregarded by a court: if it is longer that six months the decision on whether is should be taken into consideration depends on the circumstances. It will not necessarily bar a divorce on the ground of unreasonable behaviour.

Desertion

Desertion means the 'withdrawal from cohabitation without reasonable cause with the intention of permanently ending the cohabitation without the agreement of the other party'.

This is rarely used as a basis for divorce. A petition on the grounds of behaviour is usually regarded as more satisfactory. Alternatively, after the two people have been apart for two years or more, a petition on the grounds of two years separation and consent is often preferred to the more aggressive petition claiming desertion.

Separation

The remaining two grounds involve a set period of separation.

When are people treated as living apart? Two people may live entirely separate lives under the same roof. Living apart means living in separate households which usually necessitates living separate lives, for example not sleeping, eating or socialising together. If people remain under the same roof a court may require oral evidence to prove that there has been a sufficient separation even if the petition is undefended. The court will adjourn a case for the hearing on oral evidence before considering whether to grant a divorce on the ground of separation.

NULLITY

On certain limited grounds a marriage may be declared a nullity. Where this happens the marriage will either be void from the start – treated as if it had never place ('void ab initio') – or voidable but not void until a court declares it to be. Which of these options is declared depends on the basis of the petition.

Void from the start

A marriage is void from the start if:

- The two people are not respectively male and female or are 'within the prohibited degrees of relationship' which means closely related
- One of the parties is under the age of 16
- One or both of the parties is aged 16 or 17 and a necessary consent is withheld
- The marriage ceremony does not take place in accordance with the statutory requirements
- One of the parties is already married (there are specific laws relating to polygamous marriages)
- In the case of a marriage celebrated before 1971, lack of consent would probably make the marriage void (this is only of academic interest)

A voidable marriage

This applies when:

- The marriage has not been consummated owing to the incapacity of either person to consummate it. Consummation means 'ordinary and complete intercourse'; sterility or the use of contraceptives will not be regarded as preventing consummation
- The marriage has not been consummated owing to the wilful refusal of the respondent to consummate it. 'Wilful refusal' means a settled and definite decision come to without just excuse. A temporary refusal that could be overcome by tact and persuasion is not sufficient
- Either person did not validly consent to the marriage as a result of duress, mistake, unsoundness of mind or otherwise
- At the time of the marriage either person, though capable of giving a valid consent, was suffering (whether continuously or intermittently) from mental disorder. The disorder must come within the meaning of the Mental Health Act 1983 and be of a kind or to such an extent that it makes the person unfit for marriage. To be fit for marriage a person must be capable of living within a marriage and carrying out the ordinary obligations and duties of marriage

- The respondent was suffering from a transmittable venereal disease at the time of the marriage. The petitioner must show that he or she did not know that the respondent was suffering from the disease at the time of the marriage
- The respondent was pregnant by some person other than the petitioner at the time of the marriage. Again, the petitioner will have shown that he was ignorant of the pregnancy at the time of the marriage.

A general defence to a petition on one of the above grounds is to show that the petitioner had an opportunity to avoid the marriage (ie declare it void), but lead the respondent to believe that the petitioner would not seek to do so and that it would therefore be unjust to the respondent to grant the decree.

INITIATING JUDICIAL SEPARATION, DIVORCE AND NULLITY

The starting point in any of these three proceedings is a petition. This is a document that is sent to the other party to the marriage and sets out:
- the full names of the parties
- the date and place of the marriage
- where the parties both live and what they do
- if they have any children (and if so their names and dates of birth)
- the grounds for the divorce/judicial separation or nullity
- the orders that are sought (ie divorce, judicial separation or nullity).

In most cases the petition is 'served', or sent, through the court by post. It may come as an unpleasant surprise to the respondent; that unpleasantness can only be added to by the weight of formal documentation that comes with the petition. The three other documents are:
- a notice of proceedings
- an acknowledgment of service
- a statement of arrangements in respect of the children.

Notice of proceedings This a formal document in a standard form. It is long and wordy, but needs to be read. Its purpose is to tell the respondent what needs to be done. In particular it explains:
- That the acknowledgment of service must be sent back and reach the court within seven days of the respondent receiving the notice of proceedings. This time limit is very short but needs to be observed
- That if a solicitor is to be instructed, that solicitor should be handed the documents 'at once'
- How the acknowledgment of service is to be completed
- The time limits that apply if the petition is to be defended (see page 41)
- The forms to be used if the court is to be asked to make orders in respect of childre.
- How a financial claim may be made.

Acknowledgement of service This is the formal document which records that the petition has been received. It requires the respondent to answer the following questions:
- Have you received the petition delivered with this form?
- On which date and at what address did you receive it?
- Are you the person named as the respondent in the petition?
- Do you intend to defend the case?
- Do you consent to a decree being granted? (see page 41, When can a petition be defended)
- Do you object to paying the costs of the proceedings? If so, on what grounds?
- Do you agree the proposals in the statement of arrangements? If the respondent does not, counter proposals may be sent back to the court with the acknowledgment of service.

The acknowledgment of service also asks questions about polygamous marriages.

It must be signed in the circumstances described in paragraph 12a of the form, particularly if the respondent is acting without a solicitor.

Statement of arrangements Another long document which sets out in detail the proposals that the petitioner makes for the children. The details include:
- where the children will be living
- where they will be educated and who will pay any school fees
- what arrangements will be made for childcare
- what arrangements will be made for maintaining the children
- what arrangements will be made for the children to have contact with the parent with whom they are not living
- whether the children have any specific problems with their health
- whether the social services are involved with the children or whether there have been any court proceedings in respect of the children
- whether the parents are prepared to discuss any disagreements with a conciliator.

Once these three documents have been sent back to the court, the next step for the respondent to take will depend upon whether it is intended that the petition should be defended.

Defended divorces (see also page 41)
It is rare that a court is asked to decide in contested proceedings whether there are sufficient grounds for a divorce. This is because it is generally recognised that, where one person in a marriage says that the marriage is over, there is little point in spending large amounts of money fighting over that issue.

If the respondent does intend to defend the petition, an 'answer' must be filed with the court within 29 days of receiving the notice of proceedings. An answer is a formal document that 'pleads' the defence to the petition. Respondents who miss this time limit may find themselves divorced against their wishes, although a court may give a person more time, if the time limit is missed by mistake. This power to extend time should not generally be relied on.

An answer is a formal document that needs special drafting; it should not be attempted by a person without legal training.

Undefended divorces

If the petition for divorce is not to be defended, proceedings for judicial separation and divorce will follow under what has become known as the 'special procedure' or, in the case of divorce, the 'quickie divorce' procedure.

The special procedure or quickie divorce follows the steps below once the initial paperwork has been returned to the court:

- The petitioner files a written request for the judge 'to give directions for trial' ie they ask that a district judge considers the paperwork
- The petitioner files an affidavit (a document that the petitioner swears is true) in a standard form, which, amongst other things, confirms that the contents of the original petition are true
- The district judge puts the case forward for consideration of whether there should be a divorce/judicial separation, in legal language he 'enters the case in the special procedure list'
- The district judge considers the documents and, if 'satisfied that the petitioner has sufficiently proved the contents of the petition and is entitled to a decree', gives a written certificate to that effect. It is at this stage only that a court will consider whether the original divorce petition shows sufficient grounds for a divorce or judicial separation
- The district judge sends out a notice to the petitioner and respondent telling them the date set for granting the decree nisi in divorce or the decree of judicial separation. Neither person has to attend court for pronouncement of the decree nisi, unless they disagree about who should pay the costs of the divorce, in which case they will have to attend court to deal with those arguments
- A decree absolute is granted either at the request of the petitioner six weeks after the decree nisi is made (the petitioner can do this by filing a standard form with the court) or at the request of the respondent three months after the date upon which the petitioner might have applied for the decree absolute. This application is made after notifying the petitioner thereby giving the petitioner the opportunity to oppose it (which the petitioner might do, for instance, because the finances had not been resolved).

In the rare cases where there is a petition for nullity the case is sent to a judge for a hearing on evidence about whether a decree should be made.

When can a petition be defended?
A petition can be defended on the grounds that the facts upon which it is based are not true. For example, the respondent (we will assume it is a man) may argue that he has not committed the alleged adultery; or that he has not behaved as his wife alleges: or if he has behaved in the alleged way, she can still reasonably be expected to live with him: or that he has not deserted his wife or lived apart from her for the stated period. He may deny that he has failed to consummate the marriage.

In addition there are two important grounds for defending and delaying a divorce where it is based on separation:

Outstanding financial issues Where the petition is based on two years separation and consent, or five years separation, the respondent may formally apply to the court to hold up the decree absolute until the financial issues are sorted out. This brings pressure on the respondent to make sensible financial proposals at an early stage and may persuade him into agreeing to do something that the court cannot order him to do (such as taking out an insurance policy in favour of his wife so as to protect her in the event of his death).

Grave financial or other hardship Where the petition is based on five years separation, a court may refuse a decree of divorce on the grounds that dissolving the marriage will cause the respondent to suffer grave financial or other hardship. An example of grave financial hardship may be the potential loss of the widow's/widower's pension if the petitioner were to die before the respondent. An example of 'other' hardship might be the social ostracism that a decree of divorce might cause to a woman as a result of her cultural origins. The respondent will also have to show that it would be wrong to dissolve the marriage in any or all of such circumstances.

Cross-decrees
Sometimes people decide that they should divorce or obtain a judicial separation against each other. They may feel that it is unfair for one person to instigate the proceedings. If this is the case they can issue 'cross petitions' and obtain 'cross-decrees' eg, she divorces him for his behaviour and he divorces her for adultery. Although this is seen by some as 'levelling the playing field', it is likely to prove more costly than a simple undefended petition.

Why is the basis of the divorce important?
A divorce decree is an order of the court and in subsequent proceedings the basis upon which it was obtained cannot be denied. For example, if a divorce is obtained on the grounds of adultery, it cannot be said later on that the adultery did not take place. Particular allegations within the petition for divorce may be challenged later on. For instance, allegations about the respondent's behaviour to the children can be challenged in proceedings concerning the children. However, it is difficult to challenge all the allegations in a petition after a decree has been made on it because someone will ask, 'What was the basis for the decree, if all the allegations are untrue?'

If the respondent is going to permit the divorce to proceed undefended but does not accept some of the allegations in the petition for divorce, there needs to be a carefully worded letter to the petitioner explaining the respondent's response to those particular allegations.

PROPOSALS FOR REFORM

At the time of writing there are proposals for the reform of the divorce law, which have not yet been approved by Parliament. The main features of the reforms are:
- People will be expected to resolve financial and child-related issues before they are divorced
- Mediation will play a far greater role in divorce proceedings. Mediation is not the same as 'reconciliation'. It is a process whereby

people are encouraged to discuss the issues that arise on divorce or separation and resolve those issues by discussion with the help of trained mediators. Mediation is regarded as a far better way of resolving disagreements than the more adversarial court system; in most instances mediation can diminish the hostility and expense of separation or divorce
- Divorce will be possible after a period of reflection. The government proposes that the period should be one year. During that period the two people will be expected to consider whether the marriage can be saved and, if not, what should be done about the children and finances
- The present grounds for divorce – adultery, behaviour and two periods of separation, will be abolished – a divorce will be possible on the basis that the marriage has broken down irretrievably and the requisite period of reflection has passed.

CHAPTER 4

Finances

This chapter examines what the law says and does on the issue of distributing of the family's finances between spouses and former spouses in the event that a marriage breaks down and the result is a divorce, judicial separation or a decree of nullity. The financial provisions relating to children are considered in the next chapter.

WHAT IS FAIR?

The essence of the law in England and Wales in financial decision making is to try to achieve what is fair between the two people who were married in the light of their circumstances. First consideration is given to the welfare of any child of the family who has not yet reached the age of 18. There is no simple fraction, formula or other hard and fast rule that can be applied to decide what a person is entitled to in terms of money or property. Often people think that any property will automatically be divided fifty-fifty; although in some instances this proportional split may be fair, in others it will not – such an approach could leave a wife and children on the street.

THE COURT'S INVOLVEMENT

Most couples sort out the financial arrangements without having to ask a judge to impose a financial solution. However, even where the couple agree about the financial arrangements, they may still wish to record the details of any agreement between them, formally, using a consent order of the court. Therefore, in most instances there is only a limited role for the court to play in the finances.

Full and frank disclosure

It is quite impossible to achieve a fair financial solution if the two people involved do not know each others' circumstances. Therefore the law imposes a duty of 'full and frank disclosure' on them both. This means that they must both disclose all information which is relevant to the question of how the finances should be re-arranged, including the full extent of their respective financial positions (financial assets should not be hidden or understated) and any intention to remarry or cohabit following separation from their former partner.

If a person fails, in a significant way, to observe this duty, there is a risk that any financial agreement between the two people or court order may be set aside by the court. The duty of full and frank disclosure is therefore an important one.

Its existence helps to reinforce both to lawyers and those directly involved in making financial decisions that there is a two-stage approach:
- What are the relevant financial and other circumstances of both parties?
- How should the finances be re-distributed in order to achieve a fair solution for each member of the family in the light of those circumstances?

What does a court take into account?

A court must consider specific factors when deciding on financial matters (in lawyers' language, when deciding matters of ancillary relief). Those factors are laid down in the relevant Act of Parliament (section 25 of the Matrimonial Causes Act 1973). They also need to be considered where the two people are trying to achieve an agreed solution to their financial differences.

The first consideration is the welfare of any minor children of the family. The other factors are:
1 The income and earning capacity that each of the parties has or is likely to have in the forseeable future. This includes, in the case of earning capacity, any increase which the court thinks the parties can be reasonably expected to take steps to acquire.

2 The property and other financial resources that each of the parties has or is likely to have in the foreseeable future.
3 The financial needs, obligations and responsibilities which each person has or is likely to have in the foreseeable future.
4 The standard of living enjoyed by the family before the breakdown of the marriage.
5 The age of both parties and the duration of the marriage.
6 Any physical or mental disability of either party.
7 The contributions to the welfare of the family which both parties have made or are likely to make in the foreseeable future, including any contribution by looking after the home or caring for the family.
8 The conduct of both persons, if, in the opinion of the court, it would be inequitable to disregard it.
9 In the case of divorce or nullity, the value to each person of any benefit (for example a pension) which they will lose the chance of acquiring if the marriage is dissolved or annulled.

1 Income and earning capacity

Income includes all income that either person has or is likely to have in the foreseeable future. There is no element of income that is ignored.

A person's income is assessed at the time the issue is being considered either by the court or the persons themselves. The position is not frozen at the time of separation although previous patterns of income may help to identify current incomes. The reasons for increases in income following separation may also have to be considered in deciding what is fair: for example, if one party in a childless marriage has worked hard following separation but the other has not, this might affect the overall fairness of the position, particularly if the separation took place a long time ago.

Income in the foreseeable future can be more difficult to identify. Where a person is in a stable job, future income will be easy to find out but the issue invariably becomes more complicated over the earning capacities of both parties, particularly where a wife has not been in paid employment during the marriage. To what extent can she be expected to either go out and get a job or retrain?

The answers to these questions depend on what is reasonable in the circumstances of the family involved. For instance, to suggest that a woman with three children under the age of 5 should take on full-time work may be absurd. Equally, to suggest that a healthy childless woman in her thirties is unemployable may not be a reasonable argument.

Particularly difficult questions arise where a woman in her late forties or early fifties has given up her former career in order to care for the children – to what extent can she be expected to earn an income following a divorce, now that the children are no longer dependent?

Save for obvious cases, where one party plainly cannot work, the expectation is that both parties will do what is 'reasonable'. This involves:
- making enquiries about what work is available by looking in newspapers or going to the local job centre
- deciding whether the work is suitable – it may be difficult to argue that the former wife of a rich Earl should stack shelves in a supermarket
- identifying how much income the work would produce.

State benefits are also taken into account. This has a bearing for people who are caught in the 'poverty trap' – people who would be in a much worse position if they worked and lost state benefits. This may arise, for example, where a wife is left in the matrimonial home which has a high mortgage secured against it; while claiming state benefits she may get help with paying the mortgage and thereby avoid the losing the home.

2 Property and other resources

This involves identifying everything that the couple has or is likely to have by way of capital or other financial resources.

The starting point is to draw up a full list of the capital assets. In order to make the list accurate it may be necessary to obtain:
- valuations of the home and other houses, land or property (unless there is an agreement about the values)
- a mortgage statement for any mortgages or charges affecting the properties

- surrender values (or sale values) for any insurance or endowment policies.

Some individual issues that may arise over the identification of property include:

Businesses Particular difficulties arise where one person has an interest in a business. Should the business be valued ? If so, on what basis?

There are three main types of business:
- a company, in which the ownership lies with the shareholders
- a partnership, in which a number of people join together into a firm or partnership
- a sole trader, who trades under a trade name (eg John Y O'Y, trading as Ever Late Supplies).

Precise valuations of businesses may be impossible to achieve. Where valuations are attempted they can always be challenged and valued differently by someone else. This is because it is very difficult indeed to predict what any one person would pay for a business, particularly a small business that depends almost entirely on the reputation of its present owner for its success.

Where a husband and wife separate it is rarely sensible to suggest that the business should be sold because in most cases it will continue to be the main source of income for the family, even after a separation. If there is no suggestion that the business should be sold the courts will not encourage attempts at precise valuations. Instead the courts are likely to need the following:
- a general and broad assessment of the profits and assets of the business – its financial standing
- an assessment of what income and capital is available to the person with the interest in the business in the light of that business interest – the liquidity of the person.

If selling the business is a possibility, there may have to be a more thorough assessment of its value. The same is true where the couple have worked equally in the business and have an equal interest in it, for example if they were in partnership together.

Valuations or assessments of businesses are complex and should not be attempted by the untrained except in very straightforward cases. Normally, professional help from an accountant or solicitor should be obtained.

The matrimonial home The home in which the married couple lived together often represents the main capital asset of the family. However, it cannot be regarded as the same as having cash in the bank. Not only is it the family's accommodation, it may also be an important part of the family's security, particularly when there are children. There may also be significant liabilities that go with the home, not least the mortgage. Taken together, these features of the matrimonial home mean that there can be no general rule about what will happen to it after a divorce. Some of the options are:

> **The sale of the home** This may be inappropriate, for instance where there are young children and a sale would not enable both parents to be rehoused.
>
> **Transfer of the home to one of the persons** This may be an option where there are other capital assets to balance the value of the home or where there is to be a clean break.
>
> **Keeping the home on specific terms** One person may be allowed to remain in the home until certain events occur – examples of such 'property adjustment orders' are **Mesher** orders and **Martin** orders (see Glossary on pages 126 and 127 for full definitions of these orders). Mesher orders can leave the person who occupies the home at a significant disadvantage when the children reach the requisite age under the order because they may have insufficient money to buy another home at a time when the children may still need to be housed.

Inheritances When people divorce is poses the question of what account should be taken of money that has been inherited or may be inherited in the future.

Where money has been inherited already it counts as the property of that person. Its presence cannot be ignored and may be of relevance within the overall financial settlement.

Where there is a possibility that one person will inherit money or property in the future, it is very rare that a court will take it into account. This is because wills can always be changed and the amount of any future inheritance or the date upon which it will be received remains uncertain.

New partners How relevant are the financial resources of a new partner? If the husband forms a relationship with another woman, how relevant are the finances of that other woman in deciding what is fair between the husband and wife? Can the new partner be forced to reveal her/his financial position?

A new partner (we will assume it is a woman) is under no responsibility to provide for the former wife of the man with whom she lives. However, her financial position may be relevant when assessing the financial 'needs' of the husband; for instance, can a man who has set up home with a millionairess claim that he 'needs' enough to buy a house? Where the finances of the new partner are relevant, she might be forced to attend court and disclose their financial position by a witness summons or subpoena.

Other financial resources These may include:
- pensions (see page 55)
- interests under trusts, including any money that is likely to be paid under a discretionary trust
- company cars or other business perks.

3 Needs, obligations and responsibilities

'Needs' in these circumstances means the reasonable needs of each person; what is 'reasonable' will vary from case to case. For example, what is reasonable for a very rich person may not be the same as what is reasonable for a person in very poor circumstances. In many instances a primary 'need' is to make appropriate provision for the children.

Often the main 'need' is for both people to be housed. One or both persons will have to move out of the home. If rehousing is a priority it will be necessary to find out:
- the cost of suitable alternative housing
- the amount of any mortgages that are available and the probable monthly repayments
- the cost of moving into, furnishing and, possibly, renovating any new property.

Sometimes rehousing in rented accommodation is suggested as an option. However, where available, most rented accommodation is only under short-term leases which means moving regularly and this can be unsettling, particularly for young children if they have to move school every time they move house.

Council housing is another option, but satisfactory council housing is rarely available at short notice and even where it is, it may not be in the area where the family wants to live. If this option is suggested the local housing authority should be asked to confirm what is likely to be available, before any decision is made to rely on council housing.

4 Standard of living

In most cases a family's standard of living will drop as a result of separation because incomes and capital assets that were geared to meeting the expenses of one household will have to be stretched to provide for two. Therefore attempting to maintain the standard of living that existed during the marriage is often an impossible ambition. However, it is obviously necessary to take into consideration the family's way of life during the marriage when deciding how to organise the new regime after separation.

5 Age of the parties and duration of the marriage

The age of a person is obviously relevant to earning capacity, pensions and other issues. It may be unreasonable to expect a 55 year old woman to train for employment but reasonable to expect a 25 year old to do so. Pensions may be of little significance where the persons concerned are in their twenties but very relevant where they are in their fifties.

The duration of the marriage is relevant because the financial issues following a marriage of two years may be entirely different from those that arise after a marriage of 30 years. Where there are children the responsibilities arising from the marriage will be experienced for many years to come and therefore the actual duration of the marriage may not be so relevant.

Living together prior to marriage does not make the marriage any longer. However, where obligations arise out of a period of pre-marital cohabitation, such as obligations to children, this will clearly reduce the significance of the actual duration of the marriage.

In a short childless marriage, it is usual to give particular consideration to the effect of the marriage on both persons (eg what they have lost/gained collectively as a result of the marriage and how that can be reflected in the financial arrangements following divorce) as well as to the individuals' needs. Often a clean break will be thought appropriate, possibly after the party in the weaker financial position has received maintenance for a short period and any appropriate capital sum.

> **When is a marriage 'short'?** Generally speaking a marriage of under three years is regarded as short but sometimes this term is used for marriages of up to five years.

6 Disabilities

Disabilities affect many of the other considerations dealt with in this chapter. They may affect need and earning capacity.

7 Contributions

Contributions can be defined in many ways. For example caring for the children may be a very major contribution. Although the main wage earner, often the husband, may have contributed the main income of the family, he might only have been able to do so because the wife cared for the children.

Contributing financially to the marriage, although not necessarily the dominant contribution, may still be relevant when deciding what is fair between the couple. Examples of financial contributions are where the husband provided the household income or where a wife's family gave the couple the money for their family home.

8 Conduct

It is rare that behaviour influences the appropriate financial solution between a couple. The courts stress that conduct should only be taken into account where it is so significant that an objective bystander would conclude that it would be unfair to disregard it. The catch phrase used to be that conduct had to be 'gross and obvious' before a court would take it into account when deciding financial issues. The one that now appears in the Act of Parliament refers to behaviour where 'it would, in the opinion of the court, be inequitable to disregard'.

Examples of where conduct might be relevant are:
- where the wife shot the husband
- where the husband abused the children
- where a blameless husband was abandoned by a promiscuous wife for another man
- where a husband forged the wife's signature on a mortgage deed in order to raise money to provide for his girlfriend.

Before deciding to raise the issue of conduct in a divorce case, it should be remembered that conduct is only one relevant factor out of many to be considered when making decisions on finances. If one person raises the issue of conduct, the other will usually raise, or attempt to raise, issues of conduct in reply; for example, 'I went off with another man because my husband was being violent towards me'. Also, remember that raising conduct as an issue may significantly increase the cost and unpleasantness involved in sorting out the finances.

9 Pensions

Pensions have recently become the focus of considerable interest. All too often wives were losing out to a major extent after divorce proceedings because the husband would retain rights under a pension that gave him a financial security his wife did not share. This imbalance has been the subject of litigation and also of recent legislation.

Pensions raise difficult issues on divorce for many reasons:
- At the time of the divorce it may be many years before they will be received
- Pensions can rarely be treated as if they are cash in the bank, because they are tied up by the terms of the pension trust and pension legislation
- Other capital assets are usually too small to allow the person without a pension to make a capital investment in a pension scheme and therefore gain similar provision to the other spouse.

Under current law the court has to take account of the value of any benefits that either party may lose as a result of divorce or nullity. An example is where the wife would lose the possibility of receiving a widow's pension under a husband's pension if the husband were to die first. Such losses are often taken into account in a general way, for example by the wife having more of the existing capital at the time of divorce or nullity to compensate her for future loss. It may be possible to arrange for insurance to replace this benefit.

Recently a former wife was able to persuade a court that her former husband's pension fund should be varied in her favour so that she took a slice of the pension fund (that slice being paid into a pension of her own). However, this is generally regarded as a rather unusual case and does not set a precedent for all former wives.

Anyone seeking to claim a slice of a former spouse's pension will need specialist advice from a lawyer who deals with this subject.

Pensions Act 1995 In the summer of 1995, the Pensions Act 1995 was passed and is likely to come into force in 1996. Under the Act the court

will be able to decide who receives the pension benefits at the time those benefits are paid out. In particular it will be able to:
- order the spouse (or former spouse) with pension rights to make payments from the pension to the spouse without pension rights
- order the trustees or pension managers to make payments to the spouse without pension rights
- order the spouse with pension benefits to 'commute' part of their pension, which means take some of the pension benefits in the form of a lump sum and pay some of the money received from commutation to the other spouse.

COURT ORDERS

1 Maintenance Pending Suit

In the early stages of divorce it may be necessary to agree or ensure appropriate maintenance for the family while the main financial issues are being resolved. It is often at this stage that things are particularly difficult for the couple especially where they are having to pay for two households instead of one. The best way to approach this problem is for each person to draw up his or her own realistic and carefully collated list of all income received and then a list of all necessary expenditure. The lists can then form the basis for discussion on the appropriate level of any maintenance.

2 Periodical payments and a clean break

Most couples, and most courts, would prefer a clean break solution because it permits both parties to completely sever ties with each other. However, it is not true that there is a predisposition towards a clean break; for instance a former wife may need maintenance. When attempting or contemplating a clean break solution, bear the following in mind:

Periodical payments for a former spouse end on remarriage. Therefore a wife who receives a large capital settlement to compensate her for the loss of maintenance could have secured a very real advantage if she remarries within a few months or years. Once a capital settlement has been made there are only rare circumstances in which that settlement can be altered later on.

A lump sum invested in a building society or similar institution may not provide an income equivalent to maintenance. Fluctuating interest rates and the effects of inflation can reduce the amount of interest produced by savings unless the money is very well invested. This subject needs specialist financial advice.

Maintenance may be subject to variation according to the means of the persons involved. Therefore, if you are getting maintenance and your former spouse's financial circumstances diminish, yours are also likely to diminish.

A final clean break solution, that cannot be altered at a later date, is achievable only by getting a court order. The order has to be worded in a specific way which again needs specialist legal advice. Without it you could find yourself thinking that you have achieved a clean break when you have not.

Clean breaks do not have to take effect immediately. They may be deferred to a later date, for example at such time when the spouse in the weaker financial position has had an opportunity to get a better paid job. The wording of the order is all important.

Calculating maintenance When maintenance is to be paid, how is the amount calculated? The purpose of maintenance is to ensure that both the recipient and the payer have a reasonable income. What amounts to a reasonable income will obviously vary from marriage to marriage. If there is a substantial income, it may be unfair to calculate maintenance solely on the basis of the recipient's basic needs.

The best way of approaching maintenance is often to calculate how much both parties need – what their expenditure is likely to be – and then to look at a maintenance order which meets only the recipient's needs and see if this leaves the payer with a disproportionately high or low income. If it is high the order can be adjusted so that maintenance is higher. If it is low, the maintenance obligation will have to be reduced and both parties will need to reduce their expenditure.

Sometimes a court will consider what has become known as the 'one-third rule'. This suggests that a former wife who is to receive maintenance should receive it at a level that will leave her with one-third of the parties' joint net incomes (see below).

The one-third rule

Husband's net income (£25,000) + Wife's net income (£5,000) = Total joint incomes (£30,000)

£30,000 ÷ 3 = £10,000
£10,000 − £5,000 (wife's income) = £5,000

Wife's maintenance :   £5,000

In fact this is not a rule but, at best, a rule of thumb that can provide a starting point in calculating a former wife's entitlement to maintenance. It should not be applied rigidly; of much more importance must be the net effect of any maintenance order – ie what will the parties be left with if maintenance is at £X?

3 Capital orders

Capital orders are made by the court and are available to ensure that financial justice is afforded to both parties in respect of the capital that they have. A court will find out the capital that both parties have and will decide how it should be distributed between them.

Lump sums A lump sum is paid by one party in a divorce to the other. It is not simply an alternative to maintenance. A lump sum can be deferred. If it is £5,000 or more and the court orders that it is to be deferred, the lump sum will automatically 'carry' interest, that is, if the lump sum is not paid by a certain date, the payer will be liable to pay the basic sum plus interest on it from that date until it is paid. It is always worth specifically agreeing this point.

Property adjustment orders This is the other main capital order and it alters the parties' rights in a property (see page 65).

TAX

Maintenance is paid out of net or taxed income, unless the maintenance liability was settled under an order made before 15 March 1988. This means that the recipient does not pay income tax on the maintenance. The only tax relief on maintenance payments is whichever is the lesser of:
- 15 per cent of the maintenance paid
- the difference between the married man's tax allowance and the single person's tax allowance – £1,720 for 1995/6.

Capital Gains Tax

In some cases where capital orders are made, it may be necessary to consider the incidence of capital gains tax (CGT) which is charged on 'chargeable gains' accruing to an individual who is resident or ordinarily resident in the United Kingdom during a year of assessment.

The main points that separating couples need to bear in mind are:
- CGT is paid where a gain is made on the disposal (sale) of capital assets. The liability to pay CGT will fall on the person disposing of the asset
- transfer of assets between a husband and wife who are living together during the relevant year of tax assessment will not usually attract CGT
- CGT is not usually paid on gains made on the sale of a principal place of residence, such as the family home
- special Inland Revenue rules mean that it is unusual for CGT to be

payable where one divorcing spouse transfers the family home to the other.
However CGT may arise:
- where businesses or business assets are sold or transferred between former spouses (for example, if the husband takes over the wife's interest in a business partnership where the couple were operating on the basis that he pays her a lump sum – the husband is likely to pay CGT)
- where shares are cashed in
- where property other than the matrimonial home is sold or transferred between the former spouses
- where the matrimonial home includes a large amount of land.

If there is a risk that CGT may arise, the advice of an accountant should be sought to find out how much may have to be paid. All too often CGT is overlooked and people are left bearing a liability that was not taken into account at the time of the financial settlement.

BRINGING A CASE TO COURT

Most people are reluctant to go to court and manage to resolve the financial issues following divorce, judicial separation or nullity without a full court hearing. Their reluctance is a result of many factors including: the expense and slowness of litigation, the fact that it can be demeaning and also that there is no guarantee as to the outcome of a financial dispute. Ultimately a judge has discretion to do what he or she thinks is fair in accordance with established but broad legal principles.

The litigation process
Litigation starts with an application that sets out, in very broad terms, what orders are sought by the person making the application. Either party seeking an order of any sort must file his/her own application; it is not enough to rely on the fact that the other party has filed an application.

If you have remarried before making an application, you are barred from making an ancillary relief application (see page 46) after your remarriage (although remarriage does not prevent you from continuing with an application that was filed before your remarriage).

Finances Both parties are obliged to give details of their financial and other relevant circumstances in affidavits. Both parties can try to discover more details of the other's circumstances by exchanging questionnaires.

Responding If either party fails to file an affidavit or reply to a relevant questionnaire, a court order can require them to do so. If necessary a 'penal' notice will be added to the order warning the defaulting party that if they do not comply with the court's order they will be in contempt of court and may be sent to prison.

Expert evidence Valuations of property, an accountant's evidence or other expert evidence (if it is to be used) will have to be agreed or prepared in a way that permits it to be used as evidence, (ie in the form of a report that is shown to the other party's advisers well before any court hearing date). A judge is neither a valuer nor an accountant and if you cannot agree on the experts' evidence they will have to give evidence before the judge so that the judge can decide who is correct. Calling experts to give evidence is expensive – experts who disagree should be asked to speak to each other before the court hearing to see if they can resolve their differences.

Making offers Once the paperwork is in order, the parties will often exchange written offers of their proposals for settling the financial dispute. Usually neither wants the judge to know about the terms of their offer until the Judge has decided who should get what. This allows both parties to argue whatever they like at the hearing without the fear that the Judge will counter an argument with, 'You cannot argue that your former spouse should receive only £X since you have already offered more than that in your written offer of settlement'.

Offers are written in one of three ways:

On a 'without prejudice basis'. This means that a judge is not informed about the offer at any stage of the proceedings unless the terms of an offer are accepted

On a 'Calderbank' basis. These offers are headed 'without prejudice' but end with the statement that 'although this letter is written on a without prejudice basis, we reserve the right to refer it to the Judge on the issue of costs'. This means that, if the written offer is rejected, it can only be shown to the judge once it is decided who gets what. At that stage, the 'Calderbank' offer may be very relevant in deciding which party should pay the legal costs of the case. If the judge's decision is the same as or similar to the Calderbank offer the person who refused it may have to pay the legal costs of the person who made the offer from the date of the offer.

On an 'open' basis. This means that either party can refer the offer to the judge at any stage of the proceedings.

Barristers If you are going to be represented by a barrister you should have a meeting or 'conference' with him or her well before the hearing date and, usually, before any final offers to settle the case are made. Your solicitor should arrange this for you.

Keeping the court informed The hearing will usually take place before a district judge. You should always bring to the court up-to-date details of your financial position, in particular:
- three recent payslips or salary statements if you are employed
- your latest accounts and any other documentary evidence of your recent income if you are self-employed
- documentary proof of the current amounts of your savings ie the building society passbook, recent bank statements

- a recent mortgage statement showing the amount owed under any mortgages
- details of any properties that you think would be suitable for occupation by yourself or your former spouse
- details of any mortgages that are available to you.

Pre-trial reviews Before the hearing there may be a pre-trial review when the judge will want to ensure that the case is ready for hearing and see whether if the case can be settled by agreement.

The hearing If there is to be a hearing, it will normally be necessary for both parties to give evidence (see page 93 for details of how evidence is taken). At the end of the hearing the judge will give a full 'judgement', explaining what he/she has decided and why.

The right of appeal There is a right of appeal against ancillary relief orders. If the decision to issue such as order was taken in the first instance by a district judge, the appeal is then made to a circuit judge in the county court (or occasionally to a high court judge). If the original decision was made by a circuit judge or a high court judge, the appeal is made to the Court of Appeal.

Appeals are rare, because:
- they add to the costs
- an appeal is not usually a complete rehearing with the parties giving evidence afresh but proceeds on the evidence given to the district judge. The appeal is therefore often dealt with solely on the basis of the lawyers' arguments, or submissions, to the judge. There is sometimes an exception if the appeal is to a circuit or high court judge in which case new evidence may be allowed. In the Court of Appeal there are even more severe restrictions to the admission of fresh evidence
- on an appeal to a circuit or high court judge, it is necessary to explain why the district judge was wrong
- a Court of Appeal will not interfere with the decision of the judge

unless the judge was 'plainly' wrong – this would include a scenario in which the judge made a significant mistake about the law.

After the hearing After the case is over the court writes out or 'draws up' the order. The next step is for the order to be put into effect – this sometimes means that legal steps have to be taken to enforce it.

ENFORCEMENT

There are a number of methods in which orders can be enforced:

Enforcing maintenance orders

Attachment of earnings An order that the employer deducts the maintenance from the payer's income before he or she receives it.

A judgement summons When maintenance has not been paid the amount owed is recorded in a formal court document and the person in default is ordered to pay off the arrears. If the arrears are not paid, an application can be made for the person in default to go to prison.

Registering the order in the magistrates' court Payments are made through the magistrates' court, which records what has been paid. If payments fall into arrears, the person in default may have to explain why he/she should not have to go to prison for the default.

Enforcing lump sums

Garnishee orders Payments are ordered direct from a specific fund held by the other party (eg a building society account).

A charging order The amount owed is secured by way of a charge against the property of the person in default. This may be followed by an application that the property be sold.

Bankruptcy of the person in default This weapon needs to be treated with extreme caution because to make a former spouse bankrupt can have an effect on the other spouse, since a bankrupt's property is then controlled by the trustee in bankruptcy. Also a bankruptcy order may lead to other creditors claiming the bankrupt's property which in turn can leave little for the former spouse.

Distress Sending in the bailiffs to seize the goods of the person in default and sell them so as to satisfy the judgement.

Enforcing a property adjustment order
This may be enforced by the judge signing the necessary documents himself. For example, if the judge orders the home to be transferred to the other spouse, the judge may sign the necessary documents of title in place of the defaulting spouse.

CHAPTER 5

Property Issues between Cohabitees

This chapter considers how issues between former cohabitees concerning their property may be resolved.

Property ownership under the general law relating to property has been considered in Chapter 1. If cohabitees separate and need to decide what share each of them has in their home, they will need to consider some of the following points.

THE DEEDS

The deeds of the property will have to be inspected. In most cases these are held by the building society or bank who gave a mortgage on the property and a written request will be needed asking them for copies of the deeds.

Property in this country is either registered or unregistered. Ownership of a registered property is recorded at the land registry, ownership of unregistered property is not. In the case of registered property or land, the 'deed' by which the property is formally placed in the name of the owners is called a 'transfer'. In the case of unregistered property or land, the 'deed' is called a 'conveyance'. In addition to these documents there may also be a 'declaration of trust' in which the persons' beneficial interests (ie shares) in the property are declared. Often the declaration of trust is to be found in the conveyance, although it is sometimes in a separate document.

The deeds will often be lengthy documents, but what you are looking for are details of the following:
- In whose name does the property stand? Is it in joint names or only in the name of one person?
- What does the document say about the beneficial interests in the property? This is sometimes difficult for the lay-person to decipher, but the relevant bit usually begins with words like:
'to hold unto the purchasers as beneficial joint tenants' or 'to hold unto the purchasers as beneficial tenants in common as to a one quarter share to Miss Jones and as to a three-quarters share to Mr Smith...'

AGREEMENTS AT THE TIME OF PURCHASE

If the deeds of the property do not define the parties' shares in it, the next step is to consider what was expressly agreed, arranged or understood at the time the property was bought and how the owners acted upon any such agreement. This may determine the ownership of the property although it is often very difficult to remember what was said at the time the property was bought. In order to make this somewhat messy exercise more straightforward, it is always a good idea for the couple to write out

---

Example 1: agreements at the time of purchase

Mr Mine buys a property in his name and then sets up home with Miss Hopeful. Mr Mine says to Miss Hopeful, 'Although this house in being bought in my name, it belongs as much to you as it does to me'.

Miss Hopeful acts to her detriment by investing her capital in building an extension to the property because of what Mr Mine says.

Mr Mine later denies that Miss Hopeful has a share in the property.

If Mr Mine's words were written down at the time he purchased the property, he would find it difficult to maintain his position. If no record was kept of his words, then Miss Hopeful's claim may be harder to establish.

carefully what was said about property ownership at the time of purchase, so as to jolt their memories. It is worth taking time to recall this accurately.

If the deeds are silent about the claimant's share in the property and there was no express agreement or arrangement, it will be necessary to examine who paid what towards the property.

WHO PAID WHAT TOWARDS THE PROPERTY

This will need careful checking. The original conveyance file that the solicitors kept when the house was bought may help; you can ask to inspect it. alternatively, the mortgage documentation may help.

Purchase price

In the absence of a contrary agreement, the shares in the property will usually be determined according to the proportion of the purchase price each party paid. For instance, if the property was bought for £100,000 and Mr Mine paid £70,000 towards the purchase and Miss Hopeful paid £30,000, in the absence of a contrary agreement she will usually have a 30 per cent share in the property and he will have a 70 per cent share.

Mortgage

The next thing that may have to be considered is who paid what towards the mortgage and in whose name it was placed. The payment of mortgages again raises difficult issues because the courts have developed two different approaches in cases where a share in a property is claimed by a person on the basis of mortgage payments or contributions.

- A court will sometimes assess a person's share in a property by looking at the amount of capital that has been paid off the mortgage – this may be an unfair approach where there is an 'interest only' arrangement

  or

- A court may look at who is liable for what under the mortgage to form the basis of the assessment – see example 2 page 70.

Example 2: mortgage

The house is bought in the joint names of Mr Mine and Miss Hopeful for £100,000. The deeds are silent about their shares in the property and there was no express agreement about their shares. The purchase price of £100,000 was made up as follows: Mr Mine paid £70,000 from savings that he received in a divorce settlement from his former wife – this was therefore a capital contribution that he made to the purchase; the balance of the purchase price was paid by an interest only mortgage in their joint names. By the time that Mr Mine and Miss Hopeful split up the house is worth £200,000 and the mortgage remains at £30,000. Miss Hopeful's share in the property is calculated on this basis:

Her contribution to the purchase (½ the mortgage): 15 per cent
That contribution is now worth 15 percent of £200,000 =£30,000.

From her share must be deducted ½ the remaining mortgage = £15,000 so her share of the net proceeds of sale of £200,000 is £30,000 minus £15,000 = £15,000

IMPROVEMENTS

The next thing that may have to be considered is how any improvements to the property were paid for. (If the parties were engaged, special rules apply that are considered later in this chapter.) Payment for improvements will not give a person a share in the property, unless otherwise agreed or unless the owner encouraged the other party to pay for the improvements and to believe that, by making the improvements, he or she was acquiring a share in the property. This is called 'estoppel'.

TO SELL OR NOT

In dealing with this consideration, the courts will apply the principles referred to in Chapter 1, ie an order for a sale will be refused if a sale would be contrary to the original purpose of the purchase of the property.

CHILDREN

Finally, where there are children, it may be necessary to consider whether an application should be made under Schedule One of the Children Act 1989 for an order preserving the home for the children of the couple. Orders under the Children Act 1989 do not depend upon the persons' strict legal rights in the property, and may, where there are children, be used to fend off an application that their home should be sold.

ENGAGED COUPLES

People who break off engagements have an additional basis for claiming a share in a property where they have made substantial contributions to the improvement of the property in which either of the engaged couple has a beneficial interest; the contribution may be in 'money' or 'money's worth'. Where such contributions have been made the person making the contribution will acquire a share or a greater share in the property as a result of the contribution.

Where claims are based upon there having been an engagement, the claim should be brought within three years of the engagement ending.

Example 3 Engaged couples

Mr Brick bought a house for £100,000 with his own money. His fiancée, Miss Money, spent £30,000 on the property paying for an extension and, thereby, increased the value of the property by £20,000 so that the total value is £120,000. Miss Money will have a share in the property of £20,000 divided by £120,000, ie 16.66 per cent. Her share is calculated by reference to the amount that she actually spent on the property or the amount by which the property increased in value, whichever is the less. Of course if there was a contrary agreement, eg that, even though she was spending her money on the property, she would not acquire a share in it, she would not be able to claim a share.

CONTENTS AND OTHER CHATTELS

The same law that applies to ownership of 'real' property – ie land and houses – applies to ownership of contents of a house and other chattels, except that there are no formal documents such as deeds to refer to where a dispute is over chattels. Where there are disputes about contents, the best way to try to resolve them is for each of the parties to draw up lists of what they say is theirs and why. The lists can then be exchanged and attempts made to narrow or eliminate the disagreements.

CHAPTER 6
Financial Arrangements for Children

This chapter examines the responsibilities of parents to make financial provision for children. There are three main ways in which parents may be obliged to do so:
- Under the Child Support Act 1991 (CSA)
- In proceedings for divorce, judicial separation or nullity
- Under Schedule One of The Children Act 1989.

THE CHILD SUPPORT ACT 1991

This book can only give a brief account of the main features of the Act. A full summary would require a book of its own. Anyone looking for a full exposition of the workings of the Act needs to consult a specialist textbook.

The CSA came into force on 5 April 1993. Since then there have been a number of alterations to the method in which child support is calculated. No doubt there will be further alterations to its provisions. In many quarters the Act has proved deeply unpopular and there have been many criticisms of the method by which it has been enforced. The terminology and structure of the Act is complicated and leaves many people bewildered. What follows is a summary of the main features of the CSA.

The main points of the CSA
- It deals with a parent's liability to provide maintenance for a child
- It does not provide for capital payments to children: thus a lump sum or property adjustment order cannot be made under the CSA
- The liability to pay child support falls on an 'absent parent'. For the purposes of the Act a 'parent' means the mother or father of the child, not a step parent. Any dispute about parentage can be resolved by a child support officer asking a court to decide on the parentage of the child
- An 'absent' parent is one who is not living in the same household as the child concerned but lives separately from the child, for example the parent who does not have a residence or custody order in relation to the child
- The child must be an unmarried 'qualifying child' who has his home with a person who is called a 'person with care'
- To be a 'qualifying child' a child must fall into one of the following categories:

1 Under the age of 16
2 Under the age of 19 and receiving full-time education, but not advanced education, by attendance at a recognised educational establishment or elsewhere if the education is recognised by the secretary of state
3 Under the age of 18 and satisfies certain prescribed conditions.

- A 'person with care' is someone with whom a child lives and who usually provides day to day care for the child – local authorities and foster parents are excluded from this definition. Where a child spends 104 nights or more with an ' absent parent' there are specific and even more complex rules that apply to the assessment of child support.

Initiating an assessment
An assessment under the CSA may be initiated by one of the following (depending on the circumstances of the care): the 'Secretary of State' which in practice means a child support officer; a parent of the child.

Benefit Cases If a parent of a qualifying child claims or receives income

support, family credit or any other prescribed state benefit, that parent must authorise the Secretary of State to recover child support under the CSA 1991 when:
- the parent is the person with care of the child
or
- the Secretary of State requires the parent to do so

This means that, in most cases where a parent is claiming state benefits whilst looking after a child, the other parent will be forced to pay child support. This is how the State ensures that it does not bear the burden of providing for children when their parents should be doing so.

The parent with care can refuse to authorise the Secretary of State to make an assessment if that parent feels that there are 'reasonable grounds' to do so, for example, if giving authorisation would put the parent or any children living with her or him at risk of suffering harm or undue distress as a consequence. The child support officer must decide whether reasonable grounds exist. If he decides they don't, he can direct that the parent's state benefits be reduced by a prescribed amount. The parent has a right of appeal to a child support tribunal against this kind of decision by a child support officer.

Non-Benefit Cases Where neither parent is claiming state benefits, either may apply to the Child Support Agency for an assessment to be made. In many areas there is a backlog of applications that may result in significant delay before an application is processed.

How the assessment is made
The child support officer will ask both parents to give details of their financial circumstances. The parents will have to complete lengthy forms. Non-cooperation from a parent allows the child support officer to make an interim assessment which, if the parent that is not cooperating is the 'absent' parent, will be set at a deliberately high level. This strategy makes it in the interests of the defaulting absent parent to come up with the information quickly.

The assessment is made by applying strict formulae to the financial information that is provided. The precise nature of such formulae is beyond the scope of this book. There are a number of different formulae which, briefly, are:

The maintenance requirement This means the basic amount that is thought necessary to maintain a qualifying child: it is calculated in accordance with the level of income support benefits.

Assessable income of the absent parent and of the parent with care. This means the net income of each parent after deduction of allowable expenses which include: housing costs (ie rent or mortgage payments, subject to certain limitations); one half of pension payments; the basic income support allowance for a single person and any relevant children, among others. The assessable incomes of the parents are then added together and multiplied by 0.5. If the result is less than the maintenance requirement, it will represent the amount of the child support (subject to the resultant figure not offending the protected income rules, see below). If the total is more than the maintenance requirement, a different set of formulae will then have to be applied.

These different formulae involve calculating the ' basic element' and, then, the 'additional element'. The result of the calculation represents the amount of child support payable, subject to the protected income rules.

Protected income rules The protected income rules ensure that the income of the person who is paying does not fall below a protected level as a result of a child support assessment. The level of protected income is calculated by a lengthy formula.

The above represents the general method of calculation of child support in straightforward cases. Different formulae may apply, for example where there is more than one application against the same absent parent or where a child spends 104 nights a year or more with the absent parent.

Enforcing child support assessments

A valid child support assessment will be enforced by the Child Support Agency using a number of mechanisms:

A deduction from earnings order This is an order issued by the Secretary of State which instructs the employer of an absent parent to deduct the amount of the child support from the parent's earnings and pay it to the Secretary of State. This is like an attachment of earnings order (see page 64).

A liability order This can be obtained by the Secretary of State from a magistrates' court. It records the extent to which a parent has defaulted on child support payments.

Levying distress Once the Secretary of State has obtained a liability order, 'distress' is 'levied' which means that the goods of the parent in default are seized and sold to pay off the amount owed in child support.

Applying to have a defaulting parent sent to prison This happens if other methods of enforcement have failed to secure the payment of child support.

Appealing against child support assessments

If a parent thinks that a child support assessment has been calculated incorrectly, he or she can apply to the Child Support Agency for the assessment to be reviewed. The child support officer is obliged to carry out the review unless he considers that there is no basis for doing so.

If the child support officer refuses to review the assessment a parent can appeal to a child support appeal tribunal, or, in some limited circumstances, to the court. An appeal to a tribunal must be made within 28 days of notification of the child support officer's decision. An application for a review or appeal can only be made on the basis that the child support assessment has been wrongly made or calculated; it is not enough to claim that the Child Support Act is unfair.

The court's role

A court cannot make a child maintenance order where a child support officer has jurisdiction to make a child support assessment. This does not prevent the court from making capital orders for children (ie lump sum and property adjustment orders, see page 58-9 for a full explanation of capital orders.)

However, in some limited circumstances the courts still have jurisdiction to deal with child maintenance. For instance:
- where child support has been calculated in accordance with the 'additional element' formula and the court is satisfied that the absent parent should pay more than that formula suggests
- where an order is sought for the payment of school fees or for the payment of the costs of training for a trade, vocation or profession
- where the proposed payer is a step-parent
- where the person with care wants a maintenance order to be made against himself/herself – this is very rare and usually relates to an attempt to secure some tax advantages
- where the parents make a written agreement between themselves about the level of child maintenance and file that agreement with the court.

Generally speaking, where a child maintenance order was made before the Child Support Act 1991 came into force, the order will be superseded by any valid child support assessment.

ORDERS IN DIVORCE, JUDICIAL SEPARATION OR NULLITY

The court's powers to order child periodical payments (maintenance) are heavily restricted by the CSA. It can still make capital orders, such as lump sum orders or property adjustment orders. However, it is rare for a court to make capital orders in favour of children as part of a divorce settlement. The general view is that a parent's obligation is to maintain the child concerned but the available capital will be needed for the parents.

Consideration may be given to capital payments for the children in cases where there is a large amount of money available. If capital orders are made it will normally be necessary for the capital to be held in trust for the children.

Another option sometimes suggested is to transfer the family home into the names of one parent and the children. However, it is very rare indeed for a court to adopt this option because it could cause very real difficulties when the children grow up. For example one child might want to realise his or her share of the home and insist that the home is sold in order to get it. Any parents contemplating such an arrangement should think very carefully indeed before embarking upon it.

Factors the court takes into account

When considering making an order in favour of a child the court has to take into account:
- the financial needs of the child
- the income, earning capacity (if any), property and other financial resources of the child
- any physical or mental disability of the child
- how the child is being educated or trained and the future expectations of the parents regarding education and training
- the financial circumstances of the parents now and in the foreseeable future
- the needs, obligations and responsibilities of the parents now and in the foreseeable future
- the family's standard of living
- any physical or mental disabilities of the parents.

In the case of step parents the court also has to take into account:
- whether the step-parent assumed any responsibility for the child's maintenance and, if so, how much and upon what basis
- the length of time the step-parent assumed any responsibility for the child's maintenance

- if the step-parent knew whether or not the child was his or hers when he or she assumed and discharged the responsibility for the child's maintenance
- the liability of any other person(s) to maintain the child (eg the child's natural parents).

If a child maintenance order is made, the order will continue until the child reaches the age of 17, or ceases full-time education (or training), or indefinitely where there are special circumstances such as in the case of a child with a specific handicap.

SCHEDULE ONE OF THE CHILDREN ACT 1989

Under this provision of the Children Act 1989, the court may make financial orders in respect of children. The orders are made in independent proceedings which means that they are not confined to cases where there are other proceedings before a court.

The person applying for the order is either:
- the parent of the child
- a guardian of the child
- a person who has a residence order in respect of the child.

The person against whom the application may be brought is a 'parent' which is defined for the purposes of this part of the Children Act as a party to a marriage (whether subsisting or not) in relation to whom the child concerned is a child of the family — therefore a step-parent will usually be included in this definition but an unmarried cohabitee who is not a parent of the child will not.

Orders a court can make

A court can require a parent of a child either to make financial provision to the child *or* to make financial provision to the applicant (ie the other parent or guardian of the child) for the benefit of the child.

The orders are:
- child maintenance orders, subject to the restrictions imposed by the Child Support Act 1991
- secured periodical payments orders (these are very rare)
- lump sum orders
- property adjustment orders.

Factors the court takes into account
- the financial needs of the child
- the income, earning capacity (if any), property and other financial resources of the child
- any physical or mental disability of the child
- how the child is being educated or trained and the future expectations of the parents regarding education and training.
- the financial circumstances of the parents now and in the foreseeable future
- the needs, obligations and responsibilities of the parents now and in the foreseeable future

If a child maintenance order is made, the order will continue until the child reaches the age of 17, ceases full-time education (or training), or indefinitely where there are special circumstances such as a child with a specific handicap.

A maintenance order will also cease to have effect if the parents resume cohabitation for more than 6 months. Maintenance orders can, of course, be varied in order to reflect the changing needs of the parents and of the child.

Housing and schedule one of the Children Act 1989
The property rights of unmarried parents are determined by the general law relating to property. When the parents separate, this law may leave one parent with real difficulties over housing and if this parent is caring for the children of the relationship, the children may also be left homeless.

Schedule One of the Children Act 1989 has therefore become widely used as a means of ensuring that children have appropriate housing. However where, as a result of the Act a house is ordered to be provided or retained for the occupation of the children, once the children cease to be dependent, the ownership of the home usually reverts under the general law of property.

> ### Example
>
> Mr Smith and Miss Johns are not married and have two children.
>
> They live in a home that is owned by Mr Smith and in which Miss Jones has no beneficial interest (ie share).
>
> Mr Smith and Miss Jones split up and the children remain with Miss Jones in the family home. Mr Smith wants to sell the home but Miss Jones wants to stay there with the children.
>
> Miss Jones may be able to obtain an order under Schedule One of the Children Act 1989 that permits her to stay in the home while the children remain dependent. However, under the Act, Miss Jones will not herself acquire property rights in the home and when the children cease to be dependent, the property will revert to Mr Smith.

CHAPTER 7
The Children Act – 'Private Law'

The main source of the law relating to children is now the Children Act 1989; it came into force on 14 October 1991. The Act is generally regarded as being split between private law (where social services are not involved) and public law (where they are). Here we will look at private law under the Act.

THE WELFARE OF THE CHILD

When a court has to determine any question relating to the upbringing of a child, the administration of a child's property or the application of any income arising from a child's property, the court's paramount consideration is the child's welfare. This fundamental principle is applied not only by the courts but also those professionally concerned with issues relating to a child.

In section 1(3) of the Children Act 1989 there is what is sometimes called a 'welfare checklist' which itemises what a court should take into account when looking at a child's welfare. In most cases it consists of:
- the ascertainable wishes and feelings of the child concerned (considered in the light of his age and understanding)
- the child's physical, emotional and educational needs
- the likely effect on the child of any change in circumstances

- the child's age, sex, background and any characteristics of the child's which the court considers relevant
- any harm which the child has suffered or is at risk of suffering
- how capable the child's parents, or any other person to whom the court considers the question to be relevant, is of meeting the child's needs
- the range of powers available to the court under the Act in the proceedings in question.

Non-intervention

Before the implementation of the Children Act 1989 it was sometimes felt that the courts were too highly involved in matters concerning the welfare of children in cases where there were no child protection issues. As a result of this concern the Children Act ensures that court intervention is kept to a minimum and that court orders are made only when the court considers that doing so is better for the child than making no order at all. The purpose of this provision is to emphasise that people are expected to resolve disputes concerning their own children independently of the courts and only go to court when really necessary. Generally, the best people to make decisions concerning children are their parents, unless there are particular family difficulties.

Delay

Another principle that has emerged from the Children Act 1989 is that delay in resolving child-related issues should be avoided where possible. The Act specifically provides that where the courts are dealing with decisions over a child's upbringing they must take notice of the general principle that any delay is likely to prejudice the welfare of the child.

SECTION 8 ORDERS

Section 8 Orders are orders that may be made under section 8 of the Children Act 1989. They relate to contact, prohibited steps, residence and specific issues.

Who can apply for section 8 orders?

The Act differentiates between people who have a right to apply for section 8 orders and those who can apply only with the court's permission – 'with the leave of the court'. Any parent or guardian of a child and any person who has a Residence order in their favour can apply to the court for any section 8 order. Any person may apply to vary or discharge an order under section 8 if that order was made on his application.

Who is entitled to apply for Residence and Contact orders?

The following people are entitled to apply for a Residence or Contact order without obtaining the court's permission to make the application:

1 Any party to a marriage (whether subsisting or not) in relation to whom the child is a child of the family – this permits applications by most step-parents without the court's leave. A marriage is not considered to be 'subsisting' if it has been ended by divorce, nullity or death.
2 Any person with whom the child has lived for a period of at least 3 years.
3 Any person who:
  - does not have a Residence order in force in their favour but does have the consent of each person in whose favour the order was made
  - has the consent of the local authority where the authority has care of the child
  - has the consent of anyone with parental responsibility for the child.

The categories of people under 3 above usually need the court's permission to apply for a Specific Issues or a Prohibited Steps order (see page 89).

In addition, a person named in a Contact order can apply to vary that order or to discharge it.

Local authorities and local authority foster parents

There are specific limitations about the right of a local authority (ie social services) and local authority foster parents to apply for section 8 orders. Local authority foster parents who are considering applying for section 8 orders should seek legal advice before making such applications.

Obtaining the court's permission

People who do not have the right to make an application for section 8 orders without the permission of the court, which includes local authorities, local authority foster parents and children, can apply for permission. The court will take into account the following factors when deciding whether to let a person (other than the child concerned) apply for an order under section 8:
- the nature of the proposed application
- the applicant's connection with the child
- any risk there might be of the proposed application disrupting the child's life to such an extent that the child would be harmed by the application
- in cases where the child is being looked after by the local authority, the authority's plans for the child's future, and also the wishes and feelings of the child's parents.

Applications by children

Children making an application under section 8 in proceedings relating to their own welfare also come into the category of people who have to ask the court's permission to do so. Before the Act it was very rare indeed for children to initiate proceedings against their parents. It is obviously detrimental to most children to force them into the arena of conflict between their parents by allowing them to become actively involved in litigation concerning their own welfare.

When the Children Act was first implemented there was a flurry of applications by children themselves under the Act. It is specifically stated within the Children Act that where the person applying for permission to make an application for a section 8 order is the child concerned, the court may only grant permission if it is satisfied that the child has sufficient understanding to make the proposed application. Such applications are treated with such seriousness that they will generally be heard by a High Court Judge. In most circumstances the courts are reluctant to give permission for children to make applications against their parents unless it is clearly essential that this should be done.

PARENTAL RESPONSIBILITY ORDERS

These have already been considered in Chapter 1. They are not section 8 orders. Unmarried natural fathers do not automatically have parental responsibility for their children; they have to apply for an order giving them responsibility. In most circumstances the courts will grant the natural father of a child parental responsibility because it is generally regarded to be in the interests of the child that both of the child's parents should be fully recognised as having responsibility for that child. If the other parent contests an application for a parental responsibility order, the court will base its decision on:
- the degree of commitment which the father has shown to the child
- the degree of attachment between the father and the child
- the reasons of the father for applying for the order.

Where a father is having regular contact with his child it is nearly always right that he be granted parental responsibility; it may still be right where a father is not having contact with the child. It is unfortunate that whether a father does or does not have the right of parental responsibility for his children is dependent on whether he was married to the mother, rather than on how good a father he is.

Guardianship

A parent may appoint another person to have parental responsibility for a child upon the parent's death. The person appointed is a 'guardian'. The appointment must be in writing and must be dated; it must either be signed by the parent making the appointment or at that parent's direction in which case it must be signed in the presence of two witnesses. Alternatively, the appointment may be made by will. If the parent making the appointment has a Residence order in relation to the child (or if there is no other surviving parent with parental responsibility) the appointment will take effect on the death of the parent who appoints the guardian; otherwise it takes effect after the death of both parents.

The appointment of a guardian may be revoked (ie cancelled) by the person who made the appointment in one of two ways:

- by destroying the document by which the appointment was made
- by writing out a document revoking the appointment. (This document must either be signed by the person revoking the appointment or it must be signed at his direction and in his presence and also in the presence of two witnesses, each of whom 'attests the signature'.)

A person who is appointed a guardian may not wish to take up the appointment. He may disclaim the appointment by signing a disclaimer within a reasonable time of the appointment.

Residence orders

In most instances, parents who separate are able to decide where the children should live without having to come to the court. However, there are cases which are so complicated, or where the parents are so entrenched, that it is necessary for the children's future to be decided by the court.

It is sometimes thought that mothers have an advantage over fathers in residence disputes. The courts, however, have been at pains to stress that, except in the case of very young children, neither parent comes to the court with any natural advantage. The determining issue is always the welfare of the child and not any preconception of which parent is better suited to have care of the child by virtue of his or her gender.

Where a case is so finely balanced that there is no qualitative difference between the merits of what each parent is saying, a court may decide that a child should be with the mother because, in many instances, children are still cared for predominantly by the mother – but it is very rare indeed that a court decides a case on that basis alone.

Where a child is very young, the child may still be breastfed by the mother or highly dependent upon her. In those circumstances, there will have to be strong reasons to convince a court to separate the child from the mother.

Issues concerning residence matters are not restricted to parents. For instance, if one parent dies a member of the extended family may ask that the children live with him or her; a grandmother may suggest that a child's parents are unsuitable carers. The court's general approach is that it is in the interests of the child to be brought up by a natural parent rather than a member of the extended family or a family friend. Thus parents have an obvious, and understandable, advantage over others in any residence dispute relating to their own children.

Prohibited Steps orders

Prohibited Steps orders prevent a parent with parental responsibility from behaving in a certain way towards a child. For example, sometimes it is necessary to prevent the child being abducted from the country (that is from 'leaving the jurisdiction'). Another example would be an order preventing a parent from changing a child's school or changing a child's surname without the permission of the other parent.

Specific Issue orders

This is where a court has to make a decision on any aspect of parental responsibility for a child (eg if the parents cannot agree upon a specific matter concerning the child). An example of a Specific Issue order would be an order directing that a child attend a specific school where the parents can't agree or are arguing for different schools. These orders may also be used where a child is refusing to have medical treatment. Therefore the 'issue' involved does not have to relate to a disagreement between parents; it may relate to any issue regarding parental responsibility for the child.

CONTACT

Contact with an absent parent is a very important feature of a child's life. Loss of contact with a parent means that a child loses a fundamental part of its background. With this in mind, the courts consider all such loss undesirable except in exceptional cases. There have to be very strong (ie cogent) reasons before contact with the natural parents is denied.

This test of 'exceptional circumstances' and 'cogent reasons' applies where a court is deciding both whether contact should continue and whether contact should be re-introduced (for example where a father has been out of contact for some time).

Indirect contact

In very rare cases where, in the interests of the child, it is felt there should be no 'direct' or face-to-face contact, a court may order that there should be 'indirect' contact which means contact by letter, card or gift.

Supervised contact

Where there are particular difficulties over contact it may be necessary for the court to order that contact be supervised by a social worker, probation officer or by a friend of the family. The purpose of supervised contact is to ensure that the welfare of the children is properly protected during contact. Courts are often reluctant to order supervised contact for a long period of time because it is generally thought that children should have the opportunity of spending time with both parents without the intervention of third parties.

Non-compliance with a contact order

Difficult issues arise when the person with whom a child lives refuses to agree to contact between the child and an absent parent and refuses to comply with a court order. Technically, such a refusal is a contempt of court and the person in contempt can be imprisoned. However, sending a parent to prison is unlikely to make contact any easier or to help the child. Therefore, courts are extremely reluctant to contemplate sending a parent who is breaking an order to prison although some courts will consider doing so as a weapon of last resort. The court may also fine the defaulting person or order that person to pay the legal costs of any proceedings (again this is rare).

An alternative method of ensuring that a child sees both parents is to remove the child from the defaulting parent by changing the residence of the child (ie by ordering that the child should live with the parent whose contact was being frustrated). In such circumstances, more often than not the matter is brought back to court and the judge will find a way round the opposition of the defaulting parent. It is standard practice for the court to proceed on the basis that if contact is not working, a different contact arrangement should be implemented.

Grandparents

Grandparents who seek contact with their grandchildren need the permission of the court before they can make an application for contact. Many courts regard grandparents as being in a special position and think it important that the children should have contact with them. However, grandparents are not in as strong a position as a parent would be when applying for contact when making a contact application.

CHANGING A CHILD'S NAME

The Children Act specifically provides that where a Residence order is in force no one can cause the child to be known by a new surname without either the written consent of every person who has parental responsibility for the child or the permission of the court.

If a parent wishes to change the surname of a child, the parent will have to apply for a Specific Issue order (see page 89). The courts regard a change of surname as a serious matter and there has to be a good reason shown for doing so.

REMOVAL FROM THE JURISDICTION

The Children Act says that where a Residence order is in force a child cannot be removed from the United Kingdom without either the written consent of every person who has parental responsibility for the child or the permission of the court. However, this does not prevent the removal of a child from the United Kingdom for a period of less than one month by the person in whose favour the Residence Order is made. This provision is made to allow holidays to be arranged without the court becoming involved.

Where one parent wishes to remove a child from the United Kingdom permanently this inevitably raises difficult issues. Problems may arise, for instance, where a parent has married someone who lives abroad or where a parent's job involves moving to a new country. The court's will take the approach of considering the welfare of the child and how the child will be affected by removal from the jurisdiction and particularly the effect that the move would have on contact with the other parent. It also takes into account why the parent with residence wishes to remove the child. In most instances a court will be reluctant to refuse a reasonable request for the parent and child to leave the country unless it is obviously contrary to the welfare of the child.

The parent applying for permission to remove the child from the jurisdiction has to inform the court of:
- where the child would be living
- where the child would be educated
- financial arrangements for the maintenance of the child
- arrangements for the other parent to have contact with the child.

FAMILY ASSISTANCE ORDERS

The court will order a Family Assistance order where it requires a Probation Officer or a Local Authority Officer to advise, assist and, where appropriate, befriend any person named in the order. The orders are for up to six months starting on the day they are made. They permit short-term involvement by the local authority or the probation service with the family.

People who may be named in the order are:
- any parent or guardian of the child
- any person with whom the child is living or who has a Contact order in their favour and in force
- the child.

A Family Assistance order will only be made in exceptional circumstances and with the consent of every person named in the order except for the child. This is consistent with the policy of non-intervention by the courts. The purpose of such orders is to give short-term help to a family in crisis at the time when the family is having to adjust to new circumstances. An example of this would be if the parents are separating.

WELFARE OFFICERS AND WELFARE REPORTS

In almost all contested court cases concerning the welfare of children, a court will order a welfare report. This is usually prepared by a probation officer but is, occasionally, prepared by a local authority social worker. Although the welfare report is an important document in any court proceedings, it represents only the views of the welfare officer or social worker, and ultimately, cases are decided by judges.

COURT PROCEDURES

1 The person seeking orders makes an application. If the person needs permission to apply (see page 86) a written application is made for permission which is then brought before the court for consideration.
2 The evidence of the persons involved is recorded in 'statements'.
3 Following the application the court will, at an early stage, call the persons before the judge or magistrates for a 'directions' appointment where the court can 'give directions' about how the case is to progress. At this time the court will order a welfare report and, in most circumstances, investigate whether there is any prospect of the parents settling their dispute by agreement. The court may encourage the parties to attend mediation or conciliation in an attempt to resolve their differences.
4 If the case cannot be resolved by agreement, it will be listed for hearing. Before the main hearing there may be a 'pre-trial review' where the court will ensure that all the paperwork is in order and will again see if there is any prospect of the case being resolved by agreement
5 If there are things that need to be sorted out before the main hearing, (eg where a child is to live in the meantime) the court will arrange an 'interim' hearing.
6 The case will be heard by a judge or magistrates. If the only issue before the court is the amount of contact a parent should have, the hearing in the county court will take place before a district judge (as will many interim hearings). Otherwise the hearing is likely to be before a circuit judge. Complicated cases will be heard before a high court judge.

CHILDREN AGED 16 AND OVER

Although technically a person remains a child until the age of 18, the courts are very slow to make orders where children are 16 or more unless there is a good reason for doing so. The Children Act specifically provides that only in exceptional circumstances will a court make an order under section 8 which will affect a child beyond the age of 16, unless the order sought is one to vary or discharge an existing order under section 8.

CHAPTER 8
The Children Act – 'Public Law'

This chapter considers cases under The Children Act 1989, where local authorities or other outside agencies are involved in the care of children.

A LOCAL AUTHORITY'S GENERAL DUTIES

A local authority has a general duty to safeguard and promote the welfare of children in need within its area and to help the families of children in need. It can do this by providing a range and level of services appropriate to those children's needs. This includes providing accommodation for any child if:
- there is no one with parental responsibility for the child
- the child is lost or has been abandoned
- a person who has been caring for the child is being prevented (whether or not permanently and for whatever reason) from providing the child with suitable accommodation or care.

Children who are 'accommodated' by a local authority will usually be placed with local authority foster parents, or with a relative or a family friend. Only a few children are placed in institutions such as children's homes. However, the duty to accommodate children where parents are unable to look after the children does not allow a local authority to keep the children away from parents if the parents want their children back (unless the child is 16 or over and wants to stay in local authority accommodation). In order to keep children away from parents against the parents' wishes a local authority has to apply for an order. This is called a Care order.

CARE ORDERS

No Care order or Supervision order can be made in relation to a child who has reached the age of 17, or 16 if the child is married. The making of a Care order is a very serious step in the life of any child. Before a court can make a Care order it has to be satisfied that a child is suffering, or is likely to suffer, significant harm. That harm, or likelihood of harm, must be as a result of unsatisfactory standards of care being given to the child or the child being beyond the parental control.

How does a court decide whether a child is suffering or is likely to suffer significant harm?

The significant harm test is applied to each case. The test represents a set of 'threshold criteria'. The threshold must be crossed before a local authority can obtain a Care order. The local authority has to show that the harm is significant. Harm for these purposes means ill-treatment or the impairment of health or development. It would include physical, mental or emotional abuse or serious neglect. Even where the threshold is crossed, a court must also consider the welfare of the child and the welfare checklist (see Chapter 7, page pages 83-4) before it can make a Care order. Thus not only must the threshold be crossed, but it must be shown to be in the interests of the child that there should be a Care order.

Applying for a Care order

Before a Care order is made a local authority has to to file a 'care plan' setting out its precise proposals for the child. It is often necessary to involve experts such as child psychiatrists or child psychologists on matters of child welfare, and to obtain a medical report on how the child was harmed. Because it is obviously detrimental to a case if important expert evidence is withheld from the court, it is now established that all parties have a duty to disclose relevant material to the court where there is an application for a Care order, or indeed any other order under The Children Act 1989.

Sometimes an application for a Care order in made on the basis of facts which are disputed, for example in the case of alleged sexual abuse of the child by a parent. In deciding what is fact ('findings of fact') a judge will consider all the evidence and will resolve any disputes by applying the 'civil standard of proof', sometimes referred to as the 'balance of probabilities'. In order to say that something is a fact, the judge will have to decide that it is more probable than not that something has occurred. Where there are serious allegations, such as sexual abuse, there has to be a high degree of probability before a judge will decide that abuse has occurred.

Once a court has made a Care order, its role is limited to considering whether the Care order should continue (for example if there is an application to discharge the Care order) and also the level of contact that the parents and others should have with the child. The local authority is now responsible for making arrangements for the child.

CONTACT AND CARE

Under The Children Act 1989 local authorities are obliged to allow a child in care reasonable contact with the following people:
- the child's parents
- any guardian of the child
- any person who had a Residence order in their favour and in force immediately before the Care order was made
- any person who had care of the child under an order made by the High court under its inherent jurisdiction immediately before the Care order was made.

It is sometimes thought that under the provisions of a Care order a local authority has the right to decide upon the level of contact a parent should have with his or her children. This is a mistake. In fact a local authority has a duty to provide all the categories of people listed with reasonable contact with the child in care unless a court orders otherwise.

If a person entitled to contact thinks that a local authority's arrangements are unsatisfactory he can apply to the court for an order for contact or for the arrangements to be altered.

Where a local authority thinks that a person entitled to have contact with a child should not have that contact it can apply to the court for permission to refuse contact.

Supervision orders

Supervision orders put a child under the general supervision of a particular local authority. The supervision order requires the local authority to advise, assist and befriend the child. The same threshhold criteria that are involved in Care orders apply here: the criteria have to be met and the welfare checklist applied before a court can make a Supervision order.

Generally, Supervision orders are appropriate where the concerns for a child are not so grave and a Care order is not warranted. A Supervision order may impose conditions that have to be met by the parents and the child.

Police protection 'orders'

These are short-term orders which allow the police to remove a child from a dangerous environment if he or she is likely to suffer significant harm. In fact no court order is necessary for the police to take this action. The police can remove a child to suitable accommodation and keep the child there or take reasonable steps to ensure that a child is not removed from a hospital or any other place where the child is being accommodated.

The order is often a prelude to further, long-term, action by a local authority. A child cannot be kept in police protection for longer than 72 hours.

Emergency protection orders (formerly Place of Safety order)

Where this kind of order is made a child may be removed from where he or she is living or may be returned to stay where he is living if to do otherwise is likely to cause the child to suffer significant harm. An Emergency Protection order lasts initially for eight days but this can be extended by a further seven days.

Where a local authority is applying for an emergency order, the court will make the order if the authority is investigating whether the child is suffering significant harm and authorised persons, limited at this stage to local authority personnel and the NSPCC, are being refused access to the child. The emphasis, therefore, is on co-operation with social services and it is obviously unfortunate for a child to be removed from home simply because the parents will not co-operate with social workers. Parents should cooperate even if they find social workers difficult to work with.

Interim care orders

This type of order often follows an Emergency Protection order and may be made before the court considers making a 'full' Care order. An Interim Care order will be made if the court is satisfied that there are 'reasonable grounds' for believing that the threshold criteria are satisfied. The order places a child in the care of a local authority while a case is being prepared for a full hearing. The court can also make interim Supervision orders.

Secure accommodation orders

It is rarely right for children to be locked up, even when they are in care. However, in some circumstances such a step is necessary to provide protection for the child and for the community. The Children Act 1989 says that a child's liberty can only be restricted if:
- the child has a history of running away, or is likely to run away from any accommodation other than secure accommodation and if the child runs away he is likely to suffer significant harm
or
- the child is likely to injure himself or other persons if he is kept anywhere but in secure accommodation.

The aim is to ensure that children are not 'locked up' except where necessary.

A local authority has to have a court order before it is able to place a child in secure accommodation. Initially, a Secure Accommodation order may only last for three months. After that a child can be kept in secure accommodation for a further period of not more than six months at any one time. Each time an order expires, the local authority must apply to the court for it to be extended.

Child Assessment orders

In some instances a local authority may be concerned about a child but may not wish to remove it from its parents. In these cases the authority may need to carry out an assessment of the child to see how best it can help. It can then apply for a Child Assessment order which says that the child should be assessed over a period of not more than seven days. Under the order, any person who is in a position to produce the child must do so to the person named in the order, for example a social worker who will carry out an assessment. The parents must cooperate with any conditions for the assessment specified in the order.

To make a Child Assessment order the court must be satisfied that:
- a local authority has reasonable cause to suspect that a child is suffering, or is likely to suffer, significant harm; an assessment of the child's health, development or treatment is necessary to find out whether the child is suffering, or is likely to suffer, significant harm and
- that an assessment is unlikely to be made, or to be satisfactory, in the absence of a Child Assessment order.

Under a Child Assessment order a child can only be kept away from its home if the order says that this is allowed and for the period specified in the order. The child can also be kept away from home if it is necessary for the purposes of the assessment.

Guardians ad litem

The role of a guardian ad litem is extremely important because in public law proceedings the guardian ad litem is there to represent the interests of the child. This person is independent of the local authority and ensures that the court receives a full and unbiased report on matters relating to the interests of the child.

COURT PROCEDURES

1 The person seeking orders makes an application. If the person needs permission to apply (see page 86) a written application is made for permission which is then brought before the court for consideration.
2 The evidence of the persons involved is recorded in 'statements'.
3 Following the application the court will, at an early stage, call the persons before the judge or magistrates for a 'directions' appointment where the court can 'give directions' about how the case is to progress. At this time the court will order a welfare report and, in most circumstances, investigate whether there is any prospect of the parents settling their dispute by agreement. The court may encourage the parties to attend mediation or conciliation in an attempt to resolve their differences.
4 If the case cannot be resolved by agreement, it will be listed for hearing. Before the main hearing there may be a 'pre-trial review' where the court will ensure that all the paperwork is in order and will again see if there is any prospect of the case being resolved by agreement
5 If there are things that need to be sorted out before the main hearing, (eg where a child is to live in the meantime) the court will arrange an 'interim' hearing.
6 The case will be heard by a judge or magistrates. If the only issue before the court is the amount of contact a parent should have, the hearing in the County court will take place before a district judge (as will many interim hearings). Otherwise the hearing is likely to be before a circuit judge. Complicated cases will be heard before a High court judge.

These procedures are similar to those involved in private law cases except that most cases start in the Magistrates' court (called the Family Proceedings Court for these purposes). If a case is complicated or likely to take a long time, it will be transferred to the County court sitting in the nearest care centre. Particularly complex cases may then be transferred to the High court. No welfare report is necessary because the guardian ad litem and the local authority have to investigate and assess a child's welfare before proceedings reach court.

CHAPTER 9
Adoption and Fostering

ADOPTION

A child can only be adopted as a result of a court order. An Adoption order from a court gives parental responsibility for a child to the adopters. It eliminates the parental responsibility which any one person has for the child immediately before the order is made, any order made under the Children Act 1989 and any duty to pay for a child's maintenance or upbringing as a result of an agreement or court order. Thus any orders for child periodical payments are extinguished.

Adoption orders do not affect financial arrangements under a trust or under an agreement that specifically states it will survive the making of an Adoption order.

Before an Adoption order can be made, a child has to live with the proposed adopters.

If the applicant for adoption is a parent, step-parent or relative of the child or if a child is placed with the applicant by an adoption agency, or by order of the High court, a child can be adopted if it is at least 19 weeks old but only if the child has lived with one or both of the applicants for 13 weeks before the Adoption order is made. In all other circumstances, an Adoption order cannot be made unless the child is at least 12 months old and has lived at all times during the preceding 12 months with one or both of the applicants.

Only one person can apply for an Adoption order except in the case of a married couple. This means that cohabitees and homosexual couples cannot jointly adopt a child. (In such as case, one of the couple may apply for an order as a single adoptive parent.)

Applications by a married couple

A married couple applying for an Adoption order must usually both be at least 21 years of age. However, where the proposed adopters include a person who is the father or mother of the child it is sufficient that he or she is 18 years of age, so long as the husband or wife is at least 21 years of age.

At least one of the couple must live in the United Kingdom, the Channel Islands or the Isle of Man (unless the application is for a 'Convention Adoption order' which is beyond the scope of this book).

Adoptions by step-parents

Adoptions by step-parents are unusual. They are particularly rare where both natural parents are still alive because the natural parent of the same sex as the adopting step-parent would lose the status of a parent of the child; this is rarely the best solution for a child.

Where a child lives with one natural parent and a step-parent, the step-parent may be concerned about what would happen on the death of his or her own partner. One solution is that the natural parent of the couple appoints the step-parent as testamentary guardian. Another is to obtain a joint Residence order under The Children Act 1989.

Single person applications

One person can apply for an Adoption order where they are 21 years of age and not married. If the person applying to adopt is married it may still be possible to do so as a single applicant if a court is satisfied on one of the follow points:
- the other spouse cannot be found
- the spouses have separated and are living apart, and the separation is likely to be permanent
- the other spouse is either physically or mentally incapable of making an application for an Adoption order.

The applicant must live in the United Kingdom or in the Channel Islands or in the Isle of Man.

What the courts and adoption agencies take into account

A court or an adoption agency is obliged to look at 'all the circumstances', but must give first consideration to the need to safeguard and promote the welfare of the child throughout its childhood. The wishes and feelings of the child must be sought and and taken into consideration as far as is reasonably practicable.

However, the welfare of the child is not the only consideration that needs to be satisfied, particularly where one or more of the natural parents opposes the adoption.

Sometimes a court has to decide whether an Adoption order should be made against the wishes of a natural parent. For instance, a young child may have been taken into care and a local authority may propose that the child should be adopted by foster parents. In order to protect the position of the natural parents, the law prevents an Adoption order being made unless one of the following happens first:

- The child is free for adoption (see page 106 for an explanation of this phrase).
- The court is satisfied that each parent or guardian of the child freely, and with full understanding of what is involved, agrees unconditionally to the making of an Adoption order whether or not they know the identity of the proposed adopters
- The court dispenses with the agreement of the parents or guardians to the adoption.

Dispensing with parent's and guardian's agreement

A parent's or guardian's agreement can be dispensed with on specific grounds. A 'parent' is defined in this context as anyone who has parental responsibility for the child under the Children Act 1989. Therefore a father who does not have parental responsibility (eg a father who is not married to the mother and who has not obtained a Parental Responsibility order or a Parental Responsibility agreement) is not included.

The specific grounds for dispensing with a parent's or guardian's agreement are:
- if the parent or guardian cannot be found or is incapable of giving agreement
- if the parent or guardian is withholding his agreement unreasonably
- if the parent or guardian has persistently failed, without reasonable cause, to discharge his parental responsibility for the child
- if the parent or guardian has abandoned or neglected the child
- if the parent or guardian has persistently ill-treated the child
- if the parent or guardian has seriously ill-treated the child.

Freeing for adoption
This is a method used by local authorities to prepare the way for a child to be adopted. The authority applies for a court order which then allows it to place a child for adoption with prospective adopters knowing that the natural parents' consent to the making of an Adoption order is no longer necessary. The idea is to make the position of the prospective adopters more straightforward.

Before a child may be freed for adoption, the parents of the child must either agree to the Freeing order, or the agreement of the parents must be dispensed with by a court's order. A court may dispense with a parent's agreement on the same criteria as listed above.

The court will also consider the circumstances of a father who is not married to the mother in order to ensure that he has no intention of applying for a Parental Responsibility order or a Residence order. Equally, if he were to make such an application the court would ensure that it would be likely to be refused

At any time after 12 months from the making of a Freeing order, the child's natural parents may apply for it to be revoked on the ground that they wish to resume parental responsibility under the following circumstances:
- no Adoption order has been made
- the child does not live with the person with whom he has been placed for adoption.

CONTACT IN ADOPTION

The court has power to impose a condition on an Adoption order, for instance, requiring the prospective adopters to allow contact between the child and a member of the child's natural family (or, indeed, with anybody else). However, it is very rare indeed that a court will impose conditions of this sort unless the prospective adopters agree. There is a growing trend to regard contact with natural parents as beneficial to children, even after adoption, although the individual circumstances of each child have to be considered.

FOSTERING

When parents are unable to look after children, it is necessary for someone else to do so. This usually involves foster parents. If it were not for foster parents many children would be forced to live in children's homes or similar institutions. They would be deprived of the experience of family life which many regard as fundamental to a child's welfare.

Fostering can occur in one of three ways:
- by arrangement of the local authority (social services)
- by arrangement of a voluntary organisation
- by private arrangement.

Local authority fostering

A local authority may assume responsibility for a child either because the parents accept that they are unable to care for the child and ask the local authority to do so, (the technical term is 'accommodating' the child with the authority) or because a court order places a child in its care (under a Care order).

The decision to place a child with foster parents must be taken after consideration is given to the wishes and feelings of the child, the child's parents, anyone with parental responsibility for the child and anyone whose wishes and feelings the authority considers relevant, for example an older sibling.

Other considerations include:
- taking account of the child's religion, racial origin, cultural and linguistic background
- trying to place a child with a relative, friend or other person connected to the child if this is possible and compatible with the child's welfare
- trying to arrange for a child to be placed near its home
- trying to arrange for brothers and sisters to be kept together
- promoting contact between the child and the child's parents, friends and relatives unless this is not reasonably practical or contrary to the child's welfare.

Foster parents are either classed as short-term, which means that a placement is intended to last for between six and nine months, or long-term, which means that they look after children on a settled and long-term basis. They are paid a foster carers allowance to help with the costs of fostering.

Becoming a foster parent People wishing to be foster parents need specific training. A foster child can test an adult's parenting ability to the limit and may also cause tension with the other children in the foster home. If you wish to be a foster parent, contact your local social services.

Voluntary organisations

Certain voluntary organisations are approved for the purposes of placing foster children. These organisations have legal requirements attached to them that are laid down in the Children Act 1989. A local authority has a duty to ensure that any organisation placing foster children is satisfactorily safeguarding and promoting the foster child's welfare.

Private fostering

A child is considered as being privately fostered if the child is under the age of 16 (18 if the child is disabled) and is being cared for, or is living with, someone other than a parent, a person with parental responsibility or a relative. Legally, a child is not privately fostered if the person caring for the child has done so for less than 28 days and does not intend to continue for a longer period.

If you are intending to foster a child privately you have to give notice to the local authority not less than six weeks and not more than thirteen weeks before you actually receive the child. However, this does not apply where the fostering arrangement is an emergency.

In emergencies, the foster parent has to notify the local authority within 48 hours of the foster arrangements beginning. Failure to do this may be a criminal offence.

Once a local authority is notified that fostering arrangements have begun, it must satisfy itself that the child is being appropriately looked after. The normal limit for the number of foster children that a foster parent may take on is three, unless the children are all siblings or unless the local authority permits the foster parent to take on more.

CHAPTER 10

What Happens on Death?

THE IMPORTANCE OF WILLS

When a person dies there will inevitably be a high degree of distress suffered by those who were close to that person. That distress can only be increased by any financial hardship and uncertainty that arises because the dead person did not leave a valid will.

A will is an important document. In the writing of a will it is obviously important that it be made effective and that it achieves what the dead person wanted. It should also be borne in mind that the sorting out of the problems that arise when a will is badly drafted can also be a heavy and expensive burden for those left behind.

Although, in cases where there is not a great deal of money, it is possible to make a 'home-made' will, if you have any doubts about how to draft one you should get proper advice. There are a number of books that are available from most book-sellers that will help you and give information on certain formalities that have to be observed when drafting a will. However, as the contents and circumstances surrounding each persons affairs are likely to be different, in many instances it will be far better to get specific advice upon your own specific will. Your family solicitor will be able to give you that advice.

The estate

A will determines what happens to the estate of the deceased, after debts and liabilities have been met. A person's estate comprises property, money and belongings - everything they own. When a person dies without leaving a will, he dies 'intestate', and is referred to as 'an intestate'.

INTESTACY

There are specific rules that apply to who gets what from an intestate's estate. The pecking order is lengthy (it is set out in section 46 of The Administration of Estates Act 1925). For instance:

1 If the intestate dies leaving a widow (or widower) the latter will have the whole of the residuary estate as long as there are no:
- children
- parents
- brothers or sisters of 'the whole blood' (ie full brothers or sisters - not half brothers or half sisters)
- nephews or nieces of the whole blood.

2 If the intestate dies leaving a widow/er and also children, the residuary estate is divided as follows:
- The widower takes the personal chattels (ie personal possessions) and a fixed net sum out of the estate (the amount of the fixed sum is laid down in statutory 'instruments'- ie rules – at present £200,000). The net sum is free of death duties and costs and is paid with interest from the date of death
- ½ the rest of the residuary estate is held in trust for the widower during the widower's life (on death their half share goes to the children); ½ the residuary estate goes to the children.

3 If there are no children but there is a parent, a brother or sister of the whole blood, a nephew or niece of the whole blood, then the residuary estate is divided in the following way:
- the widower takes the personal chattels and the same fixed sum as is set out above and ½ the remaining residuary estate absolutely (ie not just for life)
- the other half of the remaining estate passes to the surviving parents if there are any and, if not, to the brothers and sisters of the whole blood.

4 If the intestate dies without leaving a widower the estate passes to the family in the following order of priority:
1 The children of the intestate.
2 If the intestate had no children but is survived by both parents, the

father and mother of the intestate will take the estate in equal shares.
3 If there are no children and only one parent, the parent will take the estate.
4 After this there is a list of other people who will take the estate if the intestate dies leaving no widow/er, children or parents – brothers and sisters are next on the list.

The moral of this complicated arrangement is that the rules of intestacy are rigid and may result in some relatives getting nothing. Unintentional financial hardship can be caused to others.

If you are separated from your spouse you may well want to write a new will. This is advisable particularly if you have a new family that you wish to protect.

If a person dies intestate and leaves a widow/er, that widow/er may wish to take the deceased's share in the matrimonial home as part of his/her entitlement under the law of intestacy. There are specific rules that may enable this to be done but this will require specific advice from a solicitor or other qualified person.

HOW THE ESTATE IS ADMINISTERED

A deceased person's estate is administered by his or her personal representatives who deal with the estate either in accordance with the last valid will of the deceased or in accordance with the law of intestacy. Personal representatives who administer a will are called 'executors'. Personal representatives who administer the estate of someone who dies intestate are called 'administrators'. In order to have the authority which enables them to distribute the estate the executors need to apply for a 'grant of probate' in respect of the will whereas administrators will need to apply for 'letters of administration' in respect of the estate of the deceased.

In order to do this, both should contact the local probate registry and follow the procedure that is advised.

Certain people are recognised as having priority over others to administer the estate of the deceased. The order of priority is:

1 The widower.
2 The children.
3 The father or mother.
4 The brothers or sisters (or their issue) of the whole blood.
5 Other relatives (again there is a lengthy list).

THE INHERITANCE ACT

Challenging the effect of a will or intestacy

Under the Inheritance Act (its full name is The Inheritance Provision for Families and Dependents Act 1975) certain people can challenge a will or the effects of law of intestacy. Of course, if the will is invalid, that itself gives a basis for challenging it. However, there is an additional right that is available to the following:

- the wife or husband of the deceased
- a former wife or former husband of the deceased who has not remarried
- a child of the deceased
- any person who was treated by the deceased as a child of a family to which the deceased was a party by marriage
- the deceased's cohabitee (the death must have been after 1 January 1996 and they must have lived together for at least two years before death)
- any person who, immediately before the death of the deceased, was being maintained, either wholly or partly, by the deceased.

The people included in this list can challenge a will or the law of intestacy if the will or the law of intestacy does not make reasonable financial provision for them.

An application for financial provision may take the form of maintenance, lump sums, Property Adjustment orders or orders permitting the applicant to buy property out of the estate.

'Reasonable financial provision' is defined according to the identity of the applicant. For example in the case of a widow/er it means 'such financial provision as it would be reasonable in all the circumstances of the case for a husband or wife to receive (whether or not that provision is required for his or her maintenance)'; in the case of any other applicant, it indicates 'such financial provision as it would be reasonable in all the circumstances of the case for the applicant to receive for his maintenance' – this is a more limited basis than that which applies to a widow/er since the claim is restricted to cases where the applicant is left with inadequate money on which to live.

What the court takes into account

When deciding whether or not to make an order under the Inheritance Act, and if so the nature and amount of the order, the court will look at:
- the financial resources and needs that the applicant has or is likely to have in the foreseeable future
- the financial resources and needs that any other applicant has or is likely to have in the foreseeable future
- the financial resources and needs that any other beneficiary of the estate has or is likely to have in the foreseeable future
- any obligations and responsibilities which the deceased had towards the applicant or any beneficiary
- the size and nature of the net estate
- any physical or mental disability of any applicant or any beneficiary
- any other matter that the court may consider relevant (including the conduct of the applicant or any other person).

If the applicant is the widower of the deceased extra factors are taken into consideration:
- the age of the applicant and the duration of the marriage
- the contribution made by the applicant to the welfare of the family, including any contribution made by looking after the home or caring for the family
- the financial provision that the applicant might have expected if the marriage had been terminated by divorce sooner than death.

If the application is made by a child the court will look at the manner in which the child was (or was expected to be) educated or trained. If the child is not the natural child of the deceased but was treated by the deceased as a child of the family, the court will also take into account:
- the extent, basis and duration of any responsibility that the deceased assumed for the child
- whether the deceased knew that the child was not a natural child
- the liability of any other person to maintain the child.

If the application is made by someone being maintained by the deceased immediately before his or her death, either wholly or partly, the court will look at the basis, extent and duration of the responsibility that the deceased bore for the applicant.

Time limit

Any application under the Inheritance Act needs to be made within six months of the date that representation to the estate was first taken out. The court can extend the time for applications but there needs to be a good reason before it will do so.

The Inheritance Act is not intended to encourage everyday challenges to wills. The courts will only interfere with wills and the law relating to intestacy insofar as is necessary to satisfy the requirements of The Inheritance Act 1975.

CHAPTER 11
Legal Costs

Most people who become involved in legal proceedings chose to obtain legal advice. However, that legal advice comes at a price.

The costs involved in any legal proceedings are likely to be of particular significance in family litigation. Unless legal aid is available legal costs can only be paid from the family's own resources; in most cases it is therefore vital that legal costs are kept to a minimum.

Legal costs can arise from advice that is given by a lawyer or from representation by a lawyer when a case comes to court. In some instances the costs may be covered by legal aid, although it may not cover all the costs involved.

AVOIDING COSTS

Nobody likes to waste money. It is therefore in everyone's interests that where family problems occur sensible arrangements are made with a minimum of expense. The legal system is one way of resolving the problems. However, there are other methods available that may reduce costs.

Mediation

Mediation is of increasing significance. It is sometimes referred to as 'conciliation', a term which is often confused with 'counselling' or 'reconciliation' but in fact is quite distinct from the other two.

Mediation is a process whereby people are helped to resolve disputes or problems through discussion in the presence of a mediator. The mediator helps them to identify issues, such as should the family home be sold, and to discuss these issues in a productive way.

Mediation is becoming much more frequent in divorce and separation, although it is not limited to these areas. In particular it can help where spouses cannot agree whether there should be a separation (if not, the mediator may well refer the couple for marital guidance to an institution such as Relate) or what should happen about the children (ie. contact and residence) and what financial arrangements should be made. If the couple decide to have mediation, the mediator should be in a position to advise upon the likely cost of mediation.

The proposed amendments to the divorce law give specific recognition to the value of mediation in cases of divorce or separation.

SOLICITORS AND BARRISTERS

Solicitors and barristers are both lawyers. If you need legal advice you will need to see a solicitor first. If the solicitor wants a further opinion or thinks that a barrister should do some representation in court, the solicitor may pass the case onto a barrister. In most family cases solicitors are able to represent their clients in court, they have a 'right of audience', and therefore it is a matter of choice whether a barrister should be 'instructed' to act for a client. Barristers are often instructed in difficult cases that are going to court. Where both solicitors and barristers are involved in a case this will inevitably increase the costs.

Not all lawyers do family work. If you need advice on a family matter, you will want to ensure that your solicitor has the necessary experience to handle your case effectively. The Solicitors' Family Law Association (see Useful Addresses, page 136) keeps a list of those solicitors who specialise in family work; most Citizens' Advice Bureaux (CABs) can give the names of solicitors on the list in any given area. However, it is always wise to discuss with your chosen solicitor whether he or she has the experience to handle your case.

Asking about costs

Solicitors should tell you how much their services will cost. They have a charging rate that represents the amount that they charge for each hour they devote to your case. It is sensible to ensure that you know how much a solicitor charges before asking for his advice. A solicitor's charging rate should be set out in a letter to you.

Equally, you should be told how much a barrister will cost before instructing one. Barristers' fees should be agreed by the solicitor, after consultation with the client, before the barrister's services are engaged. A 'brief fee' (ie the cost of a barrister representing a person in court) will normally be 'marked' or written on the outside of the brief.

Where a case goes on for a long time, for example where there are proceedings about money following a divorce, a solicitor must keep the client informed about the costs on a regular basis; it would be quite wrong for a client to be faced with an enormous bill at the end of a case without some clear forewarning.

Changing solicitors

You are not obliged to stick with the same solicitor or barrister. If you are dissatisfied with a lawyer you should ask to change. However, before you do so it is worth remembering that your new lawyer may have to spend time getting up to speed on your case; this will involve additional expense. Further, you should think carefully before changing solicitors shortly before a court hearing. It may not be sensible to expect a lawyer to pick up a new case at short notice. If you are receiving legal aid you may need to have the approval of the legal aid board if you want to change solicitors.

Working with your solicitor

The first stage of getting legal advice is to arrange an appointment with your solicitor. You can make the appointment by telephone or by going to the solicitor's office. You should be able to tell the solicitor the brief details of your case to ensure that you see the right person.

When you go for the first appointment take with you any documents that you think may be necessary. It may be helpful to bring a friend for support, but the solicitor will want to ensure that you have the opportunity of speaking in confidence if you need to. It is not a good idea to take children to a solicitor's office unless it is absolutely unavoidable or necessary to the case. If you intend to start divorce or separation proceedings you will need to show your solicitor your marriage certificate if possible.

After the initial interview, the solicitor will act on your instructions. In order to do this it is vital that you keep in touch with the solicitor. The solicitor will need to be able to contact you and is likely to need to see you on a number of occasions. Delay can often occur through poor communication; where this happens it simply adds to the tension of the legal process. If you are worried about your case, you should tell your solicitor about your concerns; don't allow the concerns that you have to build up.

LEGAL AID

Legal aid is controlled by the Legal Aid Board (see Useful Addresses, page 134). The rules of the legal aid scheme are laid down by Parliament.

Not all solicitors do legal aid work. You can find out which do by asking your local Citizens' Advice Bureau or by contacting the Law Society (see Useful Addresses, page 134).

Solicitors should tell you if you are eligible for legal aid and you would be well advised to discuss this matter with your solicitor at the initial interview.

Eligibility for legal aid for most types of proceedings or advice depends on how much money you have. In most cases legal aid will only be available if your case has reasonable merit, the logic being that the state should not fund hopeless litigation.

Green form advice

For those who have a low income and limited capital, 'green form' legal advice may be available. This covers initial advice and help; it does not cover representation before a court except in the case of undefended divorce proceedings. The financial limitations on the availability of green form legal aid are complex. Your solicitor will be able to advise you upon whether you are eligible.

Legal aid certificate

If you are going to be involved in court proceedings you may be eligible for legal aid to help you finance the legal costs of the proceedings. If you are eligible, the extent of your eligibility will be set out in a written certificate from the Legal Aid Board. The financial limitations for legal aid certificates are not so restrictive as those that apply to green form legal advice. You may be required to make a monthly contribution to the Legal Aid Board towards your legal aid; the amount of the contribution will depend upon the amount of money that you have.

In most cases your solicitor is under a duty to advice the Legal Aid Board about the merits of your case; this duty continues for as long as your legal aid certificate remains in force. If it becomes clear that your case no longer has any merit the solicitor must tell the Legal Aid Board.

If your case is without merit, your legal aid is likely to be withdrawn. Your legal aid may also be taken away if you refuse a reasonable offer of settlement – ie an offer made by the other party to the proceedings that your solicitor thinks that you should accept.

For some proceedings legal aid is available whatever a person's financial circumstances or the merits of a case. An example of this type of legal aid is where parents face some 'public law' proceedings under The Children Act 1989 such as care proceedings. However, the solicitor will still be required to keep the Legal Aid Board informed about what is going on in any case.

Repaying legal aid

In most cases, if you 'recover or preserve' sums of money or property as a result of proceedings covered by a legal aid certificate, you will have to repay your legal aid costs out of that money. However, this will not apply:

- if you get an order for costs against the other party to the proceedings
- if, in most family financial proceedings, you recover or preserve no more than £2,500

In many family proceedings where a person receives money or property which is intended to be used for the purposes of providing a home for that person or dependent children, it may be possible to postpone repaying legal aid. The logic of this rule is that a legally aided person should not be forced to sell a home or lose the opportunity of buying a necessary home in order to repay legal aid. However, if repayment of legal aid is postponed in this way, the legal aid costs will be secured against the home by way of a legal charge in favour of the Legal Aid Board. The effect of the charge is that if you sell the house you will have to repay the costs out of the sale proceeds together with interest on the costs. The current rate for the interest is 8 per cent per annum.

Orders for costs

The importance of both parties making offers to settle financial cases is referred to on page 61. In cases concerning the arrangements for children it is unusual for the court to make orders for costs against the party who loses. However, ultimately, costs are in the discretion of the court, which means that the court may decide what is a fair order for costs.

Changes in legal aid

Legal aid is under constant review. Each year the financial conditions vary that must be satisfied before legal aid is granted. At present some solicitors are being given more control over legal aid funding and it is likely that in the future solicitors will become stakeholders in respect of legal aid funding in a way that resembles some doctor's practices.

GLOSSARY

Throughout the book various legal phrases are used. Below is an explanation of the main ones:

CHAPTER 1

Parental responsibility The term used to acknowledge the full legal status that a parent may have towards a child. In law it means 'all the rights, duties, powers, responsibilities and authority which by law a parent has in relation to a child and his property'

Tort A civil wrong for which damages and/or an injunction may be granted by the court

Damages Compensation

Joint tenancy One way in which two or more people can own property jointly. If one of them dies the other/others will take the dead person's share automatically

Tenancy in common One way in which two or more people can own property jointly. If one of them dies the share of that person passes by his will or the law of intestacy

Right of survivorship The right whereby the dead joint tenant's share in a property passes to the surviving joint tenants

Severance of a joint tenancy Converting the joint tenancy to a tenancy in common. It is usually effected by a 'notice of severance' sent to the person wishing to sever the joint tenancy.

CHAPTER 2

Injunction An order of a court requiring a person to do (or not to do) something. Injunctions are not confined to preventing violence. They may, for instance, be granted to regulate the occupation of the home

Undertaking A formal promise to the court by someone who is involved in proceedings. It has the same effect as an injunction for the purposes of enforcement

Penal notice A notice that appears at the end of an order containing an injunction or undertaking, warning the person to whom the injunction is addressed (or the person giving the undertaking) that a breach of the injunction or undertaking may lead to imprisonment

Tort (see under Chapter 1)

Committal proceedings Proceedings that are taken when it is suggested that an undertaking or injunction has been broken. In these proceedings the court is asked to punish someone for breaking the injunction/ undertaking. In such cases the main punishment considered is imprisonment

Family Homes and Domestic Violence Bill A Bill containing proposals for the law to be made more straightforward where injunctions are sought between people who have married, have lived together or are 'associated persons'. These new proposals were expected to be introduced in the near future but may now not become law. There has been opposition to the bill form the House of Commons and, consequently, the future of the bill is undecided. At present, it seems probable that the bill will appear in an amended form, as part of the proposed reforms to the divorce law

Molest To pester or harass. It is a word used in injunction proceedings where it is suggested that one person has pestered, harassed or assaulted another

Ouster orders Orders that require a person to leave a home. The order 'ousts' the person from the home

Ex parte orders Orders of the court that are obtained in the absence of the other party, for example in emergency situations to prevent violence

Affidavits Sworn documents that contain written evidence.

CHAPTER 3

Petition The legal document that is issued by the person seeking the divorce/judicial separation etc

Petitioner The person who issues the petition (eg seeking the divorce)

Respondent The person who receives the petition

Decree absolute of divorce An order of the court that 'dissolves' (ie ends) the marriage

Decree of judicial separation An order of the court that gives legal recognition to the fact that the parties to the marriage are to live apart

Decree of nullity An order of the court by which a marriage is declared void (either void from the start or void from the date of the decree)

An answer The formal document that is filed by a respondent who wishes to 'defend' the petition (ie contend that the petition does not justify the order sought).

CHAPTER 4

Maintenance pending suit Maintenance that is ordered after a petition is issued but before the final overall financial arrangements are decided by the court or by the agreement of the parties. If temporary arrangements continue after a decree absolute, it is called 'interim maintenance'

Periodical payments Maintenance

Ancillary relief Financial provision. An order for 'ancillary relief' is an order that decides financial arrangements between spouses or former spouses

Lump sum A capital payment (eg £10,000)

Lump sum order An order that obliges one party to make capital payment to the other

Property adjustment order An order that alters the parties' rights in property, eg it may alter their shares in the matrimonial home or their rights to occupy it. Such orders are not limited to the matrimonial home

Clean break A financial arrangement whereby a party's rights of maintenance are ended by a court order. A clean break may be 'deferred'; this means that the rights of maintenance are not ended until a later date specified in the financial arrangements. A Clean Break order relates to the maintenance of the parties themselves (ie it ends the wife's or the husband's rights to claim maintenance against the other party); a legally enforceable 'clean break' conclusively ending any liability for child support or child maintenance is unlikely ever to be achieved in respect of minor children

Child of the family This is either a child of both parties to the marriage or any other child who has been treated by both parties as a child of the family (other than a foster child)

Martin order A type of property adjustment order whereby the matrimonial home is retained by the parties for the occupation of one of them (often the wife) on terms that usually provide that the home will not

be sold until the first of the following:
- the death, remarriage or cohabitation (eg for more than six months) of the party in occupation
- the party in occupation agreeing to an earlier sale or vacating the property
- a further order of the court

Mesher order   The same as a Martin order except that it includes an additional provision that the home is to be sold when the youngest child of the family reaches a certain age (often the age specified is 18), or ceases full-time education.

CHAPTER 6

CSA   The Child Support Act 1991

Child support   Maintenance (ie 'support') that is payable for a child under the CSA

Schedule One of the Children Act 1989   Part of the Children Act 1989 that permits a court to make financial orders in respect of children.

CHAPTER 7

Contact orders   Orders that require a person with whom a child lives, or is to live, to allow the child to visit or stay with the person named in the order, or for that person and the child otherwise to have contact with each other. The word 'contact' has replaced the terminology that existed before the Children Act (the previous term for contact was 'access')

Parental Responsibility orders   Orders under section 4 of the Children Act 1989 whereby a child's father (who was not married to the child's mother at the time of the child's birth) may acquire parental responsibility in respect of the child

Residence order An order deciding with whom the child is to live. Residence orders have replaced Custody orders following the implementation of the Children Act 1989

Prohibited Steps orders Orders that no step which could be taken by a parent in meeting his parental responsibility for a child, and which is of a kind specified in the order, shall be taken by any person without the consent of the court. Basically, this is an order preventing a parent with parental responsibility from behaving in a certain way in respect of the child

Specific Issues orders Orders giving directions for the purpose of determining a specific question which has arisen, or which may arise, in connection with any aspect of parental responsibility for a child. Again, basically, this means that if the parents cannot agree upon a specific matter concerning the child, they may apply to the court for a Specific Issue order

Family Assistance order An order that is made by a court which requires a Probation Officer or a Local Authority Officer to advise, assist and, where appropriate, befriend any person named in the order. These orders have effect for a period of six months beginning the day on which it is made. Family Assistance order are therefore designed to permit short-term involvement by the Local Authority or the Probation Service with the family

Welfare Officer A Probation Officer who is appointed by the court to investigate the circumstances of a child involved in any court proceedings and to report to the court on those matters

Section 8 orders Orders that may be made under section 8 of the Children Act 1989. These orders are orders for contact, prohibited steps, residence and specific issues.

CHAPTER 8

Care order An order placing a child in the care of a designated Local Authority. The consequence of a Care order is that the Local Authority is under a duty to receive the child into its care and keep the child in its care while the order remains in force. A Care order also confers on the Local Authority parental responsibility for the child and the power to determine the extent to which a parent or guardian of the child may meet his parental responsibility for the child

Interim Care order A temporary order that provides for a child to be in the temporary care of a Local Authority, whilst the application for a full Care order is being prepared for hearing

Interim Supervision order An analogous meaning to Interim Care order above

Supervision order An order putting the child under the supervision of a designated Local Authority

Police Protection order An order that permits a Police Constable, who has reasonable cause to believe that a child would otherwise be likely to suffer significant harm, to remove the child to suitable accommodation and keep him there; or to take reasonable steps to ensure that the child's removal from any hospital, or other place, in which he or she is then being accommodated, is prevented.

These are short-term orders that are intended to provide for the protection of the child; a child may be kept in police protection for no more than 72 hours. Although referred to as 'Police Protection orders' in fact no order of the court is necessary for a Police Constable to take this action

Emergency Protection order An order of the court that is usually applied for by a Local Authority where it considers there is a need for the urgent removal of a child from the environment in which the child is living. The order operates as a direction to any person who is in a position to do so to comply with any request to produce the child to the applicant (the applicant usually being the Local Authority). It authorises the removal of the child at any time to accommodation provided by or on behalf of the applicant and the child being kept there; or the prevention of the child's removal from any hospital, or other place, in which he or she is being accommodated immediately before the making of the order. It gives the applicant parental responsibility for the child

Secure Accommodation order An order permitting a Local Authority to place the child in accommodation where the child's liberty would be restricted

Child Assessment order An order that a court makes and that requires that there be an assessment of the welfare of the child

Guardian ad Litem A person appointed by the court to represent the interests of the child in any proceedings where a public law order is sought in respect of the child.

CHAPTER 10

Administrator A person who is appointed to administer the estate of a person who died without appointing executors

Executor A person appointed by a will or codicil to administer the estate of a person in accordance with a will or codicil

Personal representative A collective term used to describe either an administrator or an executor

Codicil An addition to a will

An intestate Someone who died without leaving a will

The estate The property that the dead person leaves behind

The Inheritance Act The Inheritance (Provision for Family and Dependants) Act 1975. It gives certain people the right to challenge a will or the effect of the law of intestacy in certain circumstances.

USEFUL ADDRESSES

AAA - Action Against the Abuse of Women and Girls
PO BOX 124
Chichester
West Sussex PO10 3AX

Alcoholics Anonymous
PO BOX 1
Stonebow House
Stonebow
York YO1 2NJ
Tel: 01904 644026

Asian Family Counselling Service
74 The Avenue
London W13 8LB
Tel: 0181 997 5749

British Agencies for Adoption and Fostering (BAAF)
(for information on all aspects of adoption including overseas adoption)
Skyline House
200 Union Street
London SE1 0LX
Tel: 0171 593 2000

British Association of Counselling
1 Regent's Place
Rugby
Warwickshire CV21 2PJ
Tel: 01788 578328

Catholic Children's Society
(Crusade of Rescue)
73 St Charles Square
London W10 6EJ
Tel: 0181 969 5305

The Child Poverty Action Group
1-5 Bath Street
London EC1V 9PY
Tel: 0171 253 3406

Child Support Agency
PO BOX 55
Brierley Hill
West Midlands DY5 1YL

Child Support Agency Enquiry Line
Tel: 01345 133133
(8.30 a.m. – 6 p.m. weekdays; calls charged at local rates)

Childline
Tel: 0800 1111

USEFUL ADDRESSES

Citizens' Advice Bureau
(find the address and telephone of your local branch in the telephone directory, or see NACAB)

Divorce, Mediation and Counselling Service
38 Ebury Street
London SW1W 0LU
Tel: 0171 730 2422

Families Need Fathers
(helps non-residential parents and their children)
National Administration Centre
134 Curtain Road
London EC2A 3AR
Tel: 0171 613 5060

Family Mediators Association (FMA)
PO BOX 2028
Hove, East Sussex BN3 3HU
Tel: 01273 747750

The Family Welfare Association
501-505 Kingsland Road
London E8 4AU
Tel: 0171 254 6251

General Register Office
(Births, Marriages, Deaths)
St Catherine's House
10 Kingsway
London WC2B 6JP

Gingerbread
(support for lone parents and their families)
16-17 Clerkenwell Close
London EC1R 0AA
Tel: 0171 336 8183

Good Housekeeping Institute
National Magazine Company Ltd
72 Broadwick Street
London W1V 2BP
Tel: 0171 439 5000

The Institute has been the most authoritative source of expert consumer advice since 1924. The 'Tried, Tested, Trusted' seal of approval is a guarantee to consumers and a symbol of excellence in independent research.

Jewish Marriage Council
23 Ravenshurst Avenue
London NW4 4EE
Tel: 0181 203 6311
Crisis helpline: 01345 581999

Law Society
113 Chancery Lane
London WC2A 1PL
Tel: 0171 242 1222

Legal Aid
(for leaflets and enquiries)
Information Section
85 Grays Inn Road
London WC1X 8AA
Tel: 0171 813 1000

London Rape Crisis Centre
PO Box 69
London WC1X 9NJ
Tel: 0171 837 1600 (6 p.m.-10 p.m.)

Marriage Care
Clitherow House
1 Blythe Mews
Blythe Road
London W14 0NW
Tel: 0171 371 1341

National Association of Citizens' Advice Bureau (NACAB)
Middleton House
115-123 Pentonville Road
London N1 9LZ
Tel: 0171 833 2181

National Association of Family Mediation and Conciliation Services
50 Westminster Bridge Road
London SE1 7QY
Tel: 0171 721 7658

National Consumer's Council
20 Grosvenor Gardens
London SW1W 0DH
Tel: 0171 730 0DH

National Council for the Divorced and Separated
PO BOX 519
Leicester LE2 3ZE
Tel: 01162 708880

National Council for One Parent Families
255 Kentish Town Road
London NW5 2LX
Tel: 0171 267 1361

The National Foster Care Association
Leonard House
5-7 Marshalsea Road
London SE1 1EP
Tel: 0171 828 6266

National Organisation for the Counselling of Adoptees and Parents (NORCAP)
112 Church Road
Wheatley
Oxfordshire OX33 1LU
Tel: 01865 875000

USEFUL ADDRESSES 135

**National Society for the
Prevention of Cruelty to
Children (NSPCC)**
Tel: 0171 825 2500

**Network of Access and Child
Contact Centres (NACCC)**
St Andrew's with Castlegate
Church
Goldsmith Street
Nottingham NG1 5JT
Tel: 01159 484557

Parents Against Injustice (PAIN)
(Support for wrongly accused
parents)
10 Water Lane
Bishops Stortford
Herts CM23 2JZ
Tel: 01279 656564

Parent Network
(support and education groups
for parents)
44-46 Caversham Road
London NW5 2DS
Tel: 0171 485 8535

**Principal Registry of the Family
Division**
Somerset House
Strand
London WC2R 1LP
Tel: 0171 936 6000

**The Registrar General
Adopted Children's Register**
Segensworth Road
Titchfield, Fareham
Hampshire PO15 5RR
Tel: 01329 842511
or
New Register House
3 West Register Street
Edinburgh EH1 3YT
Tel: 0131 334 0380
or
Oxford House
49-55 Chichester Street
Belfast BT1 4HL

Relate
Herbert Gray College
Little Church Street
Rugby
Warwickshire CV21 3AP
Tel: 01788 573 241

**Single Parent Links and Special
Holidays (SPLASH)**
19 North Street
Plymouth
Devon PL4 9AH
Tel: 01752 674067

**Single Parent Travel Club
(SPTC)**
37 Sunningdale Park
Queen Victoria Road
New Tupton
Chesterfield S42 6DZ
Tel: 01246 865069

**Solicitors' Family Law
Association (SFLA)**
PO BOX 302
Orpington
Kent BR6 8QX
Tel: 01689 850227

Women's Aid Federation
(refuges for women and children)
PO BOX 391
Bristol BS99 7WS
Tel: (Office) 0117 944 4411
National Helpline:
0117 942 1392

INDEX

abuse, children, 97
acknowledgment of service, divorce, 38
Administration of Estates Act (1925), 112
administrators, intestacy, 113-14, 130
adoption, 103-7
adultery, 33-4, 42
affidavits, 27, 33, 61, 125
ancillary relief, 126
answer, divorce proceedings, 39, 125
appeals:
   child support assessments, 77
   financial issues of divorce, 63-4
arrest, and injunctions, 26
assault, 21-2
assets, and divorce, 48-9
attachment of earnings, 64

bailiffs, 65
bank loans, 18
bankruptcy, 19, 65
banks, mortgages, 67
barristers:
   fees, 118, 119
   financial issues of divorce, 62
behaviour, and divorce, 34-5, 43, 54
beneficial joint tenants, 15, 17, 19
beneficial tenants in common, 15-16, 17
benefits:
   and Child Support Act, 74-5
   poverty trap, 48
bigamy, 9
bodily harm, 22
brief fees, 119
building societies, 67
businesses, and divorce, 49-50

'Calderbank' offers, 62
capital, and divorce, 48-9, 58
   see also lump sums
capital gains tax (CGT), 59-60
Care orders, children, 96-7, 107, 129
cars, company, 51
charges, on homes, 18
charging orders, lump sums, 64
chattels, property issues between cohabitees, 72
Child Assessment orders, 100, 130
child support *see* maintenance
Child Support Agency, 75, 77
children:
   adoption, 103-7
   changing the effect of a will, 116
   changing names, 91
   child of the family, 126
   Child Support Act (1991), 73-82, 127
   Children Act (1989), 15, 71, 83-94, 95-101, 103, 104, 105, 108, 121, 127
   contact with absent parents, 89-91

cruelty to, 22
and divorce, 39
and exclusion orders, 27
financial arrangements, 73-82
fostering, 107-9
guardianship, 87-8
and home ownership, 17
parents' liability for actions of, 14
personal protection orders, 26
property issues between cohabitees, 71
removal from the jurisdiction, 91-2
responsibility for, 12-14
Citizens' Advice Bureaux (CABs), 118, 120
clean break, divorce, 56-7, 126
codicils, 130
cohabitation, 9-20
and adoption, 103-4
court orders, 11
pre-cohabitation agreements, 20
property issues, 17, 67-72
rape, 22
responsibility for children, 12
violence, 25-7
committal proceedings, 27, 124
common assault, 21
common law marriage, 9
companies, and divorce, 49
conduct, and divorce, 54
consummation of marriage, 36
contact:
absent parents, 89-91

with natural parents, 107
Contact orders, children, 85, 127
contributions, and divorce, 53-4
conveyances, 67
costs, legal, 117-22
council housing, 52
county court:
Children Act, 101
injunctions, 25, 28
maintenance, 11
Court of Appeal, 63-4
court orders:
adoption, 103
child support assessments, 80-1
cohabitees, 11
divorce, 56-9, 64-5
parental responsibility, 13
courts:
and adoption, 105
Care orders, 96-7
changing the effect of a will, 115
child support assessments, 77-9, 80-1
Children Act, 84-94, 95-101
divorce proceedings, 32
financial issues of divorce, 45, 60-5
injunctions, 23-4, 25-9
maintenance orders, 10-11
undefended divorces, 40
crime, domestic violence, 21-3
cross-decrees, divorce, 42

damages, 23, 123

death, wills, 111-16
declaration of trust, 67
decree absolute, 32, 40, 125
decree nisi, 32, 40
decree of judicial separation, 125
decree of nullity, 125
deduction from earnings orders, child support, 77
desertion, 35
disabilities, and divorce, 53
divorce, 31, 32-5
   children and, 39
   cross-decrees, 42
   defended divorces, 39, 41
   financial issues, 41, 45-65
   grounds for, 33-5, 43
   initiating, 37-9
   mediation, 42-3, 118
   reform proposals, 42-3
   undefended divorces, 40-1
domestic violence *see* violence

earning capacity, and divorce, 47-8
Emergency Protection orders, children, 98-9, 129-30
endowment policies, 49
enforcement, court orders, 64-5
engaged couples, property issues, 71
estates, 131
   administration, 113-14
   wills, 111
estoppel, 70
'ex parte' injunctions, 24, 28, 125

exclusion orders, 26-7
executors, wills, 113, 130
expert evidence, financial issues of divorce, 61

Family Assistance orders, 92, 128
family credit, 75
family home *see* home
Family Homes and Domestic Violence Bill, 27, 124
Family Law Bill, 11, 25, 27, 32
Family Proceedings Court, 101
fathers:
   responsibility for children, 12-13
   unmarried, 12, 87
   see also parents
finances:
   bankruptcy, 19
   children, 73-82
   divorce, 41, 45-65
   full and frank disclosure, 46
   legal aid, 120-2
   legal costs, 117-22
   maintenance, 10-11
   pre-cohabitation agreements, 20
   pre-marriage agreements, 19
   property issues between cohabitees, 69-70
   security for bank loans, 18
   wills, 111-16
foster parents, 85-6, 95, 105, 107-9
fostering, 107-9
Freeing orders, adoption, 106

garnishee orders, 64
grandparents, contact with grandchildren, 91
grant of probate, 113
grave financial hardship, 41
'green form' advice, 120
grievous bodily harm, 22
guardian ad litem, 100, 130
guardians, children, 87-8, 104, 105-6

High court:
 Children Act, 101
 injunctions, 25
home:
 Child Support Act, 81-2
 and cohabitation, 67-72
 and divorce, 48-9, 50, 52
 exclusion orders, 26-7
 general law relating to property, 16-17
 injunctions, 25-6
 legal aid and, 121-2
 mortgages, 18
 ownership, 14-16
 property adjustment orders, 59, 65
 rights of occupation, 11
 sale of, 17
 as security, 18
 title deeds, 16, 17, 67-8
homosexuals:
 and adoption, 103-4
 violence, 24
House of Lords, 22
housing *see* home

imprisonment, failure to pay child support, 77
improvements, property issues between cohabitees, 70
income, and divorce, 47-8
income support, 74-5, 76
indirect contact, absent parents, 90
Inheritance Act (1975), 114-16, 131
inheritances, and divorce, 51
injunctions, 18, 23-4, 25-9, 124
Inland Revenue, 59-60
insurance, and divorce, 49
interest, on lump sums, 59
Interim Care orders, children, 99, 129
Interim injunctions, 24
Interim Supervision orders, children, 99, 129
interlocutory injunctions, 24
intestacy, 111, 112-13, 114, 130

joint tenancy, 15, 17, 19, 123
judgement summons, maintenance, 64
judges:
 Children Act, 101
 financial issues of divorce, 61-2, 63-4, 65
 injunction proceedings, 27-9
 undefended divorces, 40
judicial separation, 31, 32, 37, 40

land registry, 18, 67
Law Society, 120
lawyers, costs, 117, 118-20

legal aid, 117, 119, 120-2
Legal Aid Board, 120, 121, 122
legal costs, 117-22
letters of administration, intestacy, 113
levying distress, child support, 77
liability orders, child support, 77
local authorities:
    and adoption, 106
    Children Act, 95-101
    Family Assistance orders, 92
    fostering arrangements, 107-8, 109
    section 8 orders, 85-6
Looking to the Future: Mediation and the grounds for divorce, 32
lump sums, 126
    child support assessments, 78-9
    divorce, 57, 58-9
    enforcing court orders, 64
    lump sum orders, 126
    maintenance, 10-11

magistrates' courts:
    Children Act, 101
    enforcing court orders, 64
    injunctions, 26-7, 28
    maintenance, 10-11
maintenance:
    and adoption, 103
    child support assessments, 78, 79-81
    court orders, 56-8
    enforcing court orders, 64-5
    maintenance pending suit, 56, 125-6
    rights, 10-11

tax, 59-60
malicious wounding, 22
marriage, 9-20
    and bankruptcy, 19
    bigamy, 9
    definition, 9
    general law relating to property, 16-17
    injunction proceedings, 29
    judicial separation, 31, 32, 37, 40
    nullity, 31, 35-7, 41
    ownership of home, 14-16
    polygamy, 9, 36, 38
    pre-marriage agreements, 19
    rape, 22-3
    responsibility for children, 12-14
    rights, 9-14
    violence, 25-7
    see also divorce
Martin orders, 50, 126-7
Matrimonial Causes Act (1973), 46
matrimonial home *see* home
mediation, 42-3, 117-18
'mental cruelty', 34
Mental Health Act (1983), 36
Mesher orders, 50, 127
molestation, 25, 124
mortgages, 18
    and divorce, 48, 52
    property issues between cohabitees, 69-70
mothers:
    residence orders, 88
    responsibility for children, 12

see also parents
names, changing child's, 91
negligence, 23
 parents' liability for children's actions, 14
notice of proceedings, divorce, 38
notice of severance, beneficial joint tenants, 15, 123
NSPCC, 99
nuisance, 23
nullity, marriage, 31, 35-7, 41

'open' marriage agreements, 34
ouster injunctions, 25-6, 125

parental responsibilities, 12-14, 123
Parental Responsibility agreements, 13, 105
Parental Responsibility orders, 87-9, 105, 106, 127
parents:
 adoption, 103-7
 Child Support Act, 74
 Children Act, 83-94, 95-6
 contact with absent children, 89-90
 foster parents, 85-6, 95, 105, 107-9
 liability for children's actions, 14
 residence orders, 85, 88-9
partnerships, and divorce, 49
penal notice, 124
pensions, and divorce, 51, 53, 55-6
Pensions Act (1995), 55-6
periodical payments *see* maintenance

personal property, 17
personal protection orders, 26
personal representatives, estates, 130
petitioner, divorce, 31, 125
petitions, divorce, 37, 125
Place of Safety orders, 98-9
Police Protection orders, 98, 129
polygamy, 9, 36, 38
poverty trap, 48
powers of arrest, and injunctions, 26
pre-cohabitation agreements, 20
pre-marriage agreements, 19
pre-trial reviews, financial issues of divorce, 63
pregnancy, voidable marriages, 37
private fostering, 108-9
probate, wills, 113
Prohibited Steps orders, children, 85, 89, 128
property:
 charging orders, 64
 Child Support Act, 81-2
 and cohabitation, 67-72
 and divorce, 48-50
 general law relating to, 16-17
 home ownership, 14-16
 legal aid and, 121-2
 mortgages, 18
 pre-cohabitation agreements, 20
 pre-marriage agreements, 19
 sale of, 17
 as security, 18
 title deeds, 16, 17, 67-8

property adjustment orders, 59, 65, 126
punishments, breach of injunction, 27

quickie divorce, 40

rape, 22-3
registered property, 67
Relate, 118
rented accommodation, 52
Residence orders, children, 85, 88-9, 91, 97, 104, 106, 128
residuary estate, 112
respondent, divorce, 31, 125
right of survivorship, 15, 123
rights, married people, 9-14

Section 8 orders, children, 84-6, 94, 128
Secure Accommodation orders, children, 99-100, 130
security, home as, 18
separation, 31
   grounds for divorce, 35
   home ownership, 17
   initiating, 37
   judicial separation, 31, 32, 37, 40
   mediation, 118
   special procedure, 40
severance, joint tenancy, 15, 123
sexual abuse, children, 97
sexual intercourse:
   adultery, 33-4, 42
   consummation of marriage, 36
single parents, adoption by, 104-5

sole traders, 49
solicitors:
   changing, 119
   costs, 118-20
   drafting wills, 111
   'green form' advice, 120
   injunction proceedings, 27
   legal aid, 120-2
Solicitors' Family Law Association, 118
special procedure, judicial separation, 40
Specific Issues orders, children, 85, 89, 91, 128
standard of living, after divorce, 52
state benefits:
   and Child Support Act, 74-5
   poverty trap, 48
statement of arrangements, divorce, 39
step-parents:
   adoption, 103, 104
   child support assessments, 79-80
   responsibility for children, 13-14
supervised contact, absent parents, 90
Supervision orders, children, 96, 98, 129
surnames, changing child's, 91

tax:
   capital gains tax (CGT), 59-60
   maintenance, 59-60
tenants in common, 15-16, 17, 123
testamentary guardians, 104
title deeds, 16, 17, 67-8
tort, 14, 23-4, 123
trespass, 23, 24

tribunals, child support assessments, 77
trusts, 15, 51, 103

undertakings, 24, 27, 124
unmarried fathers, 12, 87
unmarried partners *see* cohabitation
unregistered property, 67

venereal diseases, 37
violence, 21-9
    as a civil wrong, 23-4
    as a crime, 21-3
    injunctions, 25-9
void marriages, 35-7
voluntary organisations, fostering arrangements, 108

welfare checklist, Children Act, 83-4
welfare officers, 93, 128
welfare reports, children, 93, 101
wills, 51, 111-16
witnesses, injunction proceedings, 27, 29